SOUND WORD

VOLUME 2

by
Mark and Denise Abernethy

A SOUND WORD, Volume 2
by Mark and Denise Abernethy
Copyright © 2004

Published by Sound Ministries International
P.O. Box 77137
Colorado Springs, CO 80970

Printed in the United States of America
International Standard Book Number: 0-9749774-2-X

We would like to dedicate this book anybody who has ever asked a biblical question that we had to answer. Those questions were instrumental in expanding our knowledge of God. . . .

To Mark —
The "king of wing", you're my best friend,
my biggest fan, you make me laugh.
Let's keep dancing like nobody's looking.

To Denise —
To the star of all my shows, you give focus to my desires, your smile lights up my world.

Acknowledgments

Andrew Wommack — thank you for your foundational teachings, especially on Spirit, Soul and Body, which literally changed our thinking. The revelation of God's grace which you so clearly express has revolutionized our relationship with God, and we are thankful for the chance to partner with you and your ministry. We appreciate the opportunities you've given us to work for you, minister with you, and also to entertain you!

Dave & Bonnie Duell — thanks for all the encouragement and telling us to "Go for it!" Dave, we still remember you telling us when we lived in Illinois to "Go West". After Denise was healed at that first meeting of yours, we knew our lives would never be the same. Your enthusiasm and joy have carried us a long way, in spite of difficult circumstances. Thank you for sharing your life experiences which have helped us to expand our vision. Bonnie, we'll always remember your words: *If you don't pursue it, the people won't get it!* Thanks for suggesting we write these books. That "bore witness" in our spirits.

Lawson & Barbara Perdue — it's a blessing to be part of your congregation. Thank you for allowing us to minister freely at your church, Charis Christian Center. We appreciate you being there for us.

Our partners who support Sound Ministries with prayers and finances—thank you for recognizing the lives that we are changing together, and helping us stomp on the devil's head!

Don & Wendy Francisco — Charlie & Jill LeBlanc What can we say! You guys are so supportive and generous. We appreciate the feedback and the time you've taken to impart into our lives. You're awesome; in heaven, we'll still be singing!

Additional resource materials:

Books:
A SOUND WORD, Volume 1

Music CDs:
Open Up The Gates!
Jumping Off The Cliff

For Further Information:

SOUND MINISTRIES INTERNATIONAL
P.O. Box 77137
Colorado Springs, CO 80970 USA
Tel/Fax (719) 683-3587

Website: www.markanddenise.com
E-mail: soundministries@msn.com

Contents

THE STORY BEHIND THE SONG

Foreword

I first met Mark and Denise in Chicago, Illinois where Mark was playing with the worship team for a church where I was ministering. We became friends and they later moved to Denver, Colorado and became a part of our local church worship team. Their enthusiastic musical ability brings life and enjoyment to audiences everywhere. Eventually, Mark and Denise joined with the ministry team of the worldwide ministry of Andrew Wommack in Colorado Springs, Colorado.

Over the years of studying the Good News Gospel, the Abernethys have honed their teaching and writing skills. And now they are publishing their first two books—books filled with the wisdom of God.

In reading these two volumes, you will find golden nuggets from the Word of God that will help you in your understanding of the Word. You will find answers for some very important questions that you have had in your mind. The Word will come alive for you and you will be blessed.

I consider Mark and Denise gifts sent by God to the Body of Christ. You will be blessed in reading the revelations that the Holy Spirit has given to them.

Dr. Dave Duell
Founder of Faith Ministries Church International and
Faith Ministries International Network
Denver, Colorado

Preface

"Hey wait, I thought you guys were musicians! What are you doing writing books?"

Well, we do play instruments, but not exclusively. Most people do a variety of things. The question is, are we what we do? Since we entered into ministry as musicians first, it seems natural that we would be categorized that way. But God puts a lot of gifts, a lot of himself, into each one of us. We think it's good and right to express what God has placed in us in every way that we find available to us.

Denise and I worked for Andrew Wommack Ministries for approximately five years in the Encouragement Department, the part of his ministry involved in making outbound contacts. As part of our responsibility, we answered questions that people had written to Andrew about various things. We began to keep a record of these answers, and we started to notice some things. Certain types of questions would come up repeatedly, falling within common areas of concern, and patterns started to emerge. For example, since Andrew ministers effectively in the area of physical healing, we had an abundance of questions regarding that.

But there was another category that we noticed and loosely termed as "doctrinal questions". These were things that Andrew Wommack Ministries didn't specifically address as a dominant focus, but they were legitimate questions that people had; we've even had some of these questions ourselves. We believe that the word of God should be able to stand up to whatever question you throw at it. The answers to these questions formed the inspiration for the publication of *A Sound Word*.

We'd like to say at the beginning that our foundation for interpreting the word of God is based on the fact that God is good, his motivation is love, his grace forms the framework for his dealings with us, and that the Bible is about the restoration of his relationship with mankind. This cannot be overstated, and is something that is non-negotiable with us. The things we have learned about the grace of God have absolutely transformed our lives. Knowing the character of God's grace makes believing him easy. We wish we had known some of these things from the very beginning.

We want to emphasize that we haven't written these things as proof texts. There are a lot of sentences that start with "I think", or "I believe"; however, this is primarily a book of answers we have written to questions we have received. We also want to add that we haven't shied away from things that are controversial. Not that we have a desire to offend, but if these issues are out there, it would be wrong to ignore them. We are also not trying to establish any particular tradition. The church holds some traditions much too dearly for its own good. Over the years, we've seen and heard a lot of strange ideas held to be untouchable truths. We'll be the first to admit that we like to take potshots at some of those. As General Schwartzkopf said, "Sacred cows make the best hamburger." If you find something in here you don't agree with, it just may be your own sacred cow!

The format of these volumes is simple with the subjects in alphabetical order. Denise wrote some, I wrote some, and some were written together. Sometimes we included the questions, sometimes we rephrased them as part of the answer. There is also a section where we comment on some of our original songs we've written (breaking the cardinal rule of the singer/songwriter—namely, *don't preach your songs!*).

It may be that the answers to some of your own questions are here—or maybe not. But real people have asked these same things, so it's likely that you know somebody who's wondering about some of this. If you don't see your questions here, they'll probably be in our upcoming volumes!

Hope this helps,

Mark & Denise

1 John 3:9 *Mark*

Whosoever is born of God doth not commit sin; for his seed remaineth in him: and he cannot sin, because he is born of God.

We received a question once from someone who made these comments: "There are many people in the church who profess to be born again in spite of continuous moral failure. To believe oneself saved and yet practice sin is possibly the worst form of self-deception. If professing born-again believers are practicing sin, they need to examine themselves to see if they are in the faith." The passage that was used to drive these points home was 1 John 3:4-10. Basically, the main idea was that you can get by with sinning occasionally since 1 John 1:9 covers that sort of thing; but if you habitually sin then you're probably not born again.

The answer lies in the nature of the born-again spirit. Ephesians 1:13 says that *we have been sealed with the Holy Ghost.* Hebrews 12:23 says that our spirits have been made perfect. Romans 8:9 says *we are not in the flesh but in the spirit.* 2 Corinthians 5:16 says, ". . . henceforth know we no man after the flesh, but after the spirit." A lot of scriptures talk about the spirit of man, which is not the same as our souls or our bodies. That is what the passage in 1 John is talking about.

In the book of 1 John, it does not say that a believer does not practice sin. It says that he does not sin— period (1 John 3:6). Verse 9 says *he cannot sin.* The common interpretation of these verses has been that a

believer doesn't practice sin; some even say in the translation that a believer does not habitually practice sin. It's
much more strict than that. *Young's Literal Translation*
says in place of *he cannot sin* that *he is not able to sin.*
Not able to sin? That's amazing! How is that possible?

Here's the explanation: John isn't talking about the
flesh when he says "whosoever abideth in him sinneth
not" because we are not in the flesh, but in the spirit
(Rom 8:9). Our spirit man is made righteous, everything
in there is of God (2 Cor 5:17-18). *Our spirit does not
sin; there is nothing in it that is not of God. It truly is not
able to sin.*

Can we still do things that the Bible classifies as sin?
Of course. Our flesh and our minds can still sin. Does it
affect us if we do? Of course it does. We need to avoid it
in every way possible. *But our spirits cannot sin.*

The traditional focus of the church has always been on
actions, simply because they are visible. Sometimes it's
the only thing that we have to go by as to whether a person is acting like he's been saved or not. But while we
are limited to looking at the external things, God looks at
the heart.

*Living according to the reality of our spiritual nature
will free us from sin more than anything else.* When we
focus on our actions, they always lead us into judging
whether they are right or not. Compared to God, our
actions will always come up short. In contrast, when we
focus on the reality of our righteous spirit, the pressure to
perform is taken away. We see ourselves for who and
what we really are, and living holy becomes what it
should be—a by-product of our true nature.

1 John 4:18   *Denise*

> *There is no fear in love; but perfect love casteth*
> *out fear; because fear hath torment. He that*
> *feareth is not made perfect in love.*

What does "perfect love casteth out fear" mean? In earlier verses of this chapter (1 John 4) we read how God is greater than the prince of this world, Satan. Verses 8 and 16 tell us that God is love. In sending his son to die for the world, he demonstrated his love to us (v9). So what kind of fear is the above verse speaking of? Fear is *expectation of judgment.* But according to the scriptures, we have already been judged. Why? Because Jesus was judged for all mankind and took our judgment upon himself when he died on the cross. Verse 17 even says that we may have *boldness* in the day of judgment. If we don't know this truth, then we won't have the confidence and boldness spoken of here—it's not based on *our* individual actions—it's about *Jesus'* actions.

Verse 18 continues by saying *fear has torment.* What is torment? Torment is punishment and infliction of extreme physical and mental pain and agony. But the same verse is prefaced with saying there is no fear in love; so whose love is it speaking of? Not ours. It would be an incredible burden for us if we would have to love perfectly before we could be rid of fear. Talk about your unrealistic expectations! This verse is speaking of *God's* perfect love for us.

Verse 19 says that we love God because *he first loved us.* What a relief it is to know that God's love for us will

3

never be based on our performance on how much *we* may try to love him. Because *he first loved us.* He beat us to the punch. He loved us while we were in sin, while we were still spiritually separated from him. Nothing you could ever do will ever be good enough to deserve his love. But *he first loved us.*

When we understand the perfect love that God has for his children, then that understanding will erase any doubt or fear of judgment you may have had. Understanding God's perfect love for you is the assurance your heart needs in order to cast out or refuse *any* fear that the devil may try to plant in your thoughts. You *have been* judged and *have been* made the righteousness of God (2 Cor 5:21). Your born-again spirit is perfectly holy (Eph 4:24). 1 John 4:17 says, ". . . , as he is, so are we in this world." Is God going to judge Jesus again? No. Will God judge a believer? No. There's a line I wrote in one of our songs, *Already Got It,* that says, *When you see me, your eyes see you.* When God looks at one of his children, he sees himself—his own spirit—in us. Allow that truth to be an anchor of hope for your soul.

A Little Lower Than Angels – Or A Little Lower Than God?

Mark

> *When I consider thy heavens, the work of thy fingers, the moon and the stars, which thou hast ordained; what is man, that thou art mindful of him? and the son of man, that thou visitest him? For thou hast made him a little lower than the angels, and hast crowned him with glory and honour.* (Psalm 8:3-5)

Concerning the word *angels* in Psalm 8:5, the Hebrew word in the original language is *elohiym*, (pronounced el-o-heem). *Strong's Concordance* has this definition: "gods in the ordinary sense; but specifically used (in the plural thus, especially with the article) of the supreme God; occasionally applied by way of deference to magistrates; and sometimes as a superlative."

It's not a question of proving the word is there—it is. The problem is more about how does one interpret the meaning of that word? It seems that to picture ourselves as a little lower than the Godhead is almost considered blasphemy in many people's eyes. How could we possibly think of ourselves as being almost on the same level as God himself? This is probably the reasoning behind its translation as *angels* in a lot of the English versions. Even in the quotation of this verse in Hebrews 2:7, the Greek word used in the text is *aggelos*, very definitely *angels*. So it seems that even the writer of the book of Hebrews backed off from saying that our position was that high.

But the word *elohiym* is translated many more times as *God* than it is as anything else. And so to say as the *Revised Standard Version* puts it, "Yet thou hast made him little less than God, and dost crown him with glory and honor . . ." is probably the more accurate way to look at the word. The most common translation of the word is very likely the best.

But then, we have to come to grips with the concept that we are the most important beings in the universe apart from God himself, even more important than the angels. We have to ask the same question David asks in the psalm, "When I look at thy heavens, the work of thy fingers, the moon and the stars which thou hast established; what is man that thou art mindful of him, and the son of man that thou dost care for him?" The answer to that question is the motivation God had when he sent Jesus to pay the price for our sins. This is why people can get absolutely head-over-heels about the love of God; it's without a doubt the best thing going!

Acts 16:31 — Claiming Salvation   *Denise*

*And they said, Believe on the Lord Jesus Christ,
and thou shalt be saved, and thy house.*
(Acts 16:31)

*Q. Is it biblical to claim someone's salvation, according
to Acts 16:31?*

A. No, that is not a scriptural thing. Simplified, if Jesus
can't "claim" anyone's salvation, we can't either. He has
made salvation a free gift to *anyone* who will believe on
him, yet he can't force us to accept his sacrifice. God has
given every person a free will; he won't make us accept
him if we don't want to.   We can either choose to believe
that Jesus paid for all our sins so we could receive his
eternal life (John 3:16), or we can choose not to accept
him or his sacrifice, and when we leave this world we can
live forever with Satan and all the wicked in the lake of
fire to be in eternal torment (Matt 13:49-50; 2 Thess 1:8-
9). I'm not trying to use this as a scare tactic, but these
are the only two options that exist.

Many people mistakenly try to use the scripture in
Acts 16:31 as a verse that promises our loved ones will be
saved as *we* "stand in the gap" or "stand in faith", believing for their salvation. We've heard from hundreds of
people who want us to pray with them to "claim" their
family members. I looked up the word *claim* in *Webster's
Ninth New Collegiate Dictionary*, which gave me several
definitions including, "to take as the rightful owner; to
ask for as a right such as an inheritance." So to claim
someone borders on manipulation and witchcraft because

you are wanting to become someone else's "rightful owner"—overriding their will with your own. That dog just won't hunt. We cannot get anyone born again by *our* faith, even if that person is part of our family or related to us. It's not that God doesn't love them, but that they need to respond to the word of God for themselves.

In Acts 16:31, Paul and Silas were saying that this jailer could be born again by believing on the Lord and the same thing would work for his family if *they* would believe. We can be encouraged to believe for salvation of our family members with scriptures such as Matthew 9:38, 2 Corinthians 4:4, Luke 10:2 and Ephesians1:17-19, but we can't claim someone's salvation with Acts 16:31.

*Mark has written more about this topic.
(See *Praying For The Lost—A Sound Word, Volume 2*)

Animals In Heaven *Mark*

Q. I love animals with all my heart. I thank God for giving them to us each day as they have brought me so much joy and love. But I have such a hard time when I see one dead by the side of the road, or abused by someone. It has always comforted me to think that they are in heaven. But I've been told that they don't go to heaven because they don't have souls. It's so hard to think of being up there without them! If they don't go to heaven, do you have advice on how I can think about them passing without shedding a tear?

A. Your note is very poignant and it points out the perspective expressed by Paul in Romans 8:22 when he writes, "For we know that the whole creation groaneth and travaileth in pain together until now." This means that the world exists in a fallen state, waiting for the manifestation of the sons of God. The death that entered in through man's sin affects everything on the planet, and it is like a great weight that causes the earth to groan like an overloaded cart. It is a picture of how things are at the moment. The whole earth wants this situation to be resolved and go back to the way it was originally designed to be. That is probably what you're picking up on.

However, this scripture is not implying that animals have eternal spirits; just that, along with everything else, they're also affected by the fallen state of the world. Our spirit is the eternal part of us that is created in the image of God; but nowhere does scripture say that animals are like us in this respect. We know animals do have souls (mind, will and emotions) and bodies, but we can't assume they have spirits—so we can't know that they will live forever. But I wouldn't be surprised if there are a lot of animals in heaven, because God is pleased with that which he creates. It would just seem natural for him to surround himself with his creation. However, Jesus did not come to die for the sins of animals.

I know that some people really hope that all animals go to heaven, though I haven't found any scriptural basis to say for certain that every animal from every age will be there to meet us. I'm not sure that desire has really been thought out. Every cockroach, every mosquito, every worm from every day of the world, along with every crow, whale, hippopotamus and rat that ever lived!? What about all the animals that missed Noah's ark? That's a lot of bio-mass!

Maybe those desires are based on people's affections for certain kinds of animals, but we don't know God's perspective on it. Maybe he has a real affection for the bacteria that break down the leaves on the forest floor, so the system will keep on functioning. We just don't know the specifics—whose animals will be there, will we even care because heaven will be so awesome, will only our *special* pets be there, etc.

Since the Bible says that the holy Jerusalem descends out of heaven (Rev 21:2, 12), I'm willing to bet that there will be an earth with animals on it. What we do know is that God loves us and provides the best for us. We also know that he is creative—infinitely creative. So whatever awaits us in eternity will be awesome.

Benefits Of Speaking In Tongues

Denise & Mark

A lot of people think that praying in tongues is a nice little thing that charismatic believers do that sets them apart as weird or flaky. Of course, people are weird enough to begin with; they don't really need much extra help. But speaking in tongues is radically different than what is normal for the world. Unfortunately, because there is so much "worldliness" in the church as a whole, a lot of Christians reject the experience, saying, "I already have the Holy Ghost, I don't need this in order to be saved," etc.

Does your salvation hinge on your speaking in tongues? No. Does it affect God's love for you? Again, no. So what's the big deal? The big deal is that you can have the opportunity and privilege to communicate with your maker—the creator of the universe—and receive his personal direction and revelation knowledge for your life.

All of the things that we have from God, such as wisdom, anointing, understanding, and direction are on the inside of us in our born-again spirit. The word of God will instruct you in a general way about who you are and what you have in the spirit, but to have specific information about how to apply all this great stuff to your own life takes more than just head knowledge. This is where the ability to pray in tongues is invaluable. As you pray in tongues, you actually increase the flow of information from your spirit to your mind.

It's hard to overstate how important that is. In 1 Corinthians 2:9-10, the Bible says that the things God has prepared for us are revealed to us by his spirit. It further says, in verse 14, that the natural man cannot receive these things because they are spiritually discerned. The only way to discern them is to get them from the spiritual dimension into the natural thought realm. The single best way to do that is through praying in tongues. Sure, you can get God's leading without praying in tongues, but you will get a whole lot more, and a lot more often, if you exercise the gift. It's like the difference between the occasional drip from a faucet and a fire hose.

For instance, Mark and I have found that an excellent way to receive direction from the Lord is to ask God about something and then just pray in tongues. Colossians 3:15 says to let the peace of God rule your heart. The *Amplified Bible* translates that as "to let the soul harmony which comes from Christ rule (act as umpire continually) in your hearts [deciding and settling with finality all questions that arise in your minds, in that peaceful state]." This means that God, who is a God of peace, will give you greater peace in one direction than another.

Let's say you have a decision to make, but you have several options to pick from. Ask God what is the best choice for you. For example, *God should I do Choice A? Is this what you want for me?* Then pray in tongues for as long as you need to in order to discern his answer by the peace he gives you, whether it takes five minutes or thirty minutes. Yes or no answers are usually easier to hear than, *Which college in the United States should I attend?* Once you have a yes or no, go on to the next question. *God, is Choice B what I should do?* Repeat this till you've exhausted your options. By all means don't forget that crucial last question: *God do you have*

something else for me that I haven't even considered?
The more you do this, the better you'll develop your
listening skills and the quicker you should be able to
receive direction from the Lord.

Praying in tongues is sort of like having a personal
morse code with God; you are actually speaking mysteries
and secret truths to him (1 Cor 14:2). Wouldn't you
rather have his wisdom operating in your life than your
own wisdom? Romans 8:27 (AMP) says that the Spirit
intercedes and meets our prayers according to and in
harmony with God's will. I don't know about you, but I
need all the help I can get!

It takes faith to pray in tongues and speak a language
you've never spoken before, but as you do so, you build
yourself up in your faith (Jude 1:20) and improve or edify
yourself (1 Cor 14:4). Isaiah 28:11-12 says that praying
in tongues is a physical refreshing. So, if you're tired
after a long day, pray in tongues for about 15 minutes.
It's like getting a boost of energy.

1 Corinthians 14:17 says praying in tongues is giving
thanks to God. Do you ever feel that in your praise and
worship to God that words can sometimes fail you? I can
say he's great and awesome and wonderful only so many
times before I start to bore even myself! That's a good
time to start praising him and singing in the spirit and
glorifying him.

Paul writes that speaking in tongues is a sign not for
the believer, but to the unbeliever on the point of believing (1 Cor 14:22). I remember years ago talking to a
woman I worked with who was asking me questions
about being a Christian. I told her that not only was this

world not my home (because heaven was), but that I also spoke a heavenly language. She scoffed at me and asked me to prove it. I started speaking in tongues to let her hear some supernatural proof, and she was astounded.

James writes that the tongue is an unruly evil, full of deadly poison (1:8). Since death and life are in the power of the tongue (Prov 18:21), we should always make a conscious effort to let words of life come forth. You've heard the adage that if you don't have something nice to say, don't say anything at all. In that case, start praying in tongues. If you feel anger rising up in you—maybe you're stuck in traffic and are feeling cranky—pray in tongues. What a wonderful answer to "road rage".

John 14:26 says that the Holy Spirit will teach us all things and bring all things to our remembrance. One time I misplaced a beautiful necklace given to me by a couple of missionaries to Mexico. I looked high and low in my house and could not find it. I was hoping I hadn't lost it and then I had a thought . . . *why don't you pray in tongues, you tell everyone else to!* I immediately started praying in tongues asking God if it was somewhere in my house, but I heard him say no. As I kept praying, a thought came to me that I had left it at a friend's house where Mark and I had spent the night several weeks before. I called Wendy on the phone and asked if she had found my necklace. She said she hadn't. I kept praying in tongues until the Holy Ghost specifically said I had placed it on a night table in that same house near the bed. I called her up a week or so later and asked the same question, to which she again replied no. A couple weeks later she called me, and I knew it was about the necklace. She said her daughter was wearing it on her neck and had found it on the night stand. Now is that cool or what?

In addition to what the Bible says, even scientific evidence supports praying in tongues as beneficial. Dr. Carl R. Peterson M.D. in Tulsa, OK, a psychiatrist, was doing research on the relationship between the brain and praying or speaking in tongues. Through research and testing, Dr. Peterson found that as we pray in the spirit, it

> ". . . causes a major stimulation in the hypothalamus. The hypothalamus has direct regulation of four major systems of the body, mainly: a) the pituitary gland and all target endocrine glands; b) the total immune system; c) the entire autonomic system; and d) the production of brain hormones called endorphins and enkephalons, which are chemicals the body produces and are 100-200 times more powerful than morphine. In summary, a very significant percentage of the central nervous system is directly and indirectly activated in the process of extended verbal and musical prayer over a period of time. This results in a significant release of brain hormones, which, in turn, increases the body's general immunity."

So, instead of focusing on bad news about the flu in winter, we should focus on God and pray in tongues!

The more we pray in tongues, the quicker we'll learn to hear from God—hear what his voice sounds like—and hopefully, make a few less mistakes along the way instead of just guessing what we should do. God wants you to hear him as clear as a bell. His sheep hear his voice, the voice of another they will not hear (John 10:4).

*We've written more about this topic. (See *Baptism Of The Holy Ghost—A Sound Word, Volume 1*)

Cain's Family   *Mark*

*Q. The Bible says that Adam and Eve were the first
people, and then Genesis 4:1-14 says they had two sons,
making it four people on the planet. After Abel's
murder, God placed a mark on Cain so no one who
found him would kill him. Who would find him besides
Adam and Eve? Then, verse 17 says Cain lay with his
wife. Where did she come from? It doesn't say that
Adam and Eve had any daughters. And even if they did,
and Cain took one of them as his wife, wouldn't that be
incest?*

A. You've drawn conclusions from scriptures that there
were only four people on the planet. In Genesis 5:4 it
says that Adam had sons *and* daughters. But in verse 3, it
says that Adam lived 130 years before he had Seth. The
mistake of your conclusion is in assuming that from Cain
and Abel to the birth of Seth there were no other children
born to Adam and Eve. Even though the scripture
doesn't say that there were other children, it also doesn't
say that there weren't.

It's most likely that between Abel and Seth, Adam had
other children. And the conclusion of Cain having one of
his sisters as his wife is the most likely one we can draw.
Even though God, in the giving of the law of Moses to
Israel later on, gave a commandment against incest, there
was no such law against it at this point in time. A lot of
things in the pre-Israelite days went on without regard to
God's law being given. It is God's standard that brothers
and sisters don't sleep together. However, in the earliest
days of the human race, particularly in Adam's family,
there was no other choice.

We hope this does not offend your sensibilities. But logically, this is the only conclusion we can draw from scripture.

Can We Command God?   *Mark*

> *Thus saith the LORD, the Holy One of Israel, and his Maker, Ask me of things to come concerning my sons, and concerning the work of my hands command ye me.* (Isaiah 45:11)

This verse does imply that we can command God about certain things. If there's even a little tendency to be religious, that thought alone starts to make a people a bit nervous. Can it really be true?

To be fair, some translations phrase this verse as a question. As an example, the *Revised Standard Version* reads like this: "Thus says the LORD, the Holy One of Israel, and his Maker: 'Will you question me about my children, or command me concerning the work of my hands?' " In looking at the various translations we currently have on hand, we find that they are evenly split. *The American Standard Version, Darby's Translation, New King James, World English Bible, Young's Literal*

Translation along with the *King James* all translate this passage as a declaration. Those that put it as a question include *The Bible In Basic English, Modern King James, Revised Standard, New International Version, The Living Bible* and *The Amplified Bible*. It's obvious that even the best scholars are divided over the intent of the original language.

So we need to see if this concept of commanding God is found anywhere else in scripture. But first, the point needs to be made that this scripture in Isaiah does not in any way imply that we have an unqualified ability to tell God what to do. To quote Andrew Wommack, "If God's grace hasn't already provided it, your faith can't get it." The thought here is not a whole lot different than going to your light switch and turning it on. We don't create electricity when we throw the switch; we are just opening a connection and directing the power to a specific location. The power has already been supplied.

If you take a look at Exodus 32:9-14, you'll find an exchange between God and Moses in which it is obvious that God was headed in a certain direction and Moses stopped him. How is it possible that anyone could tell God what to do? Yet Moses did, by bringing up the promises that God had made to Abraham, Isaac, and Jacob. In Isaiah 43:26 God says this: "Put me in remembrance: let us plead together: declare thou, that thou mayest be justified." In context of the surrounding scriptures in Isaiah, this is admittedly a sarcastic statement; and yet this is exactly what Moses did on the mountain.

In the New Testament, Jesus said, "If ye abide in me, and my words abide in you, ye shall ask what ye will, and it shall be done unto you." (John 15:7) Again, in John

14:13-14, "And whatsoever ye shall ask in my name, that will I do, that the Father may be glorified in the Son. If ye shall ask any thing in my name, I will do it." Hebrews 4:16 says, "Let us therefore come boldly unto the throne of grace, that we may obtain mercy, and find grace to help in time of need." These verses all carry the thought that we can come as sons into the throne room of God and get the things we need as part of our birthright, the things that pertain to life and godliness.

This may be a major shift in perspective for some people, but it in no way implies that we see ourselves as superior to our Father when we exercise the rights he has provided to us. These rights are ours and do not depend on this particular scripture in Isaiah 45:11. They are clearly seen in other places, and also in the loving nature of our generous Lord and Father.

Cast Your Bread Upon The Water   *Mark*

Cast thy bread upon the waters: for thou shalt find it after many days. (Ecclesiastes 11:1)

Denise and I were in a meeting one Sunday morning, and the minister who was receiving the offering started preaching from a list of 25 things that you needed to do in order for God to prosper you. I started writing them down, but after about 5 or 6 things I stopped. I got to thinking that if I had to do all those things, there wasn't any way in the world I'd get it all done. At least, not before the bucket came around!

So, mentally, I checked out, meaning my brain went somewhere else. It went over to Ecclesiastes 11:1, and I started reading about casting my bread on the waters. There was a little footnote next to the word *upon* which directed me over to the margin; and I found out that the Hebrew text literally says "upon the face of the waters".

Hmmm, I thought, as a little light bulb went off in my head, *Where have I heard that before?* My thoughts went back to Genesis 1:2, where it says that "the earth was without form, and void; and darkness was upon the face of the deep. And the Spirit of God moved upon the face of the waters." I'd seen one translation that used the word *brooding* instead of *moved.* The main thing I saw about the face of the waters that day was that it was the environment of the Holy Ghost.

I got this picture, that the Spirit of God was out there, on the face of the waters, waiting with all this potential spiritual force humming like a mighty engine, ready to go as soon as it was put into gear, ready for the spoken word of God. And this is what I heard on the inside of me— *When you cast your bread, your financial seed, out onto the face of the waters, you're surrendering that seed to the power of the Holy Ghost, who uses his creative energy to multiply it back to you, wave after wave after wave.*

I've since lost track of my little list of the 5 or 6 things out of the 25 that I was supposed to do, but the picture that God gave me about Ecclesiastes 11:1 has been with me ever since.

Christmas And Easter   *Mark & Denise*

Q. Some people say that Christmas and Easter are originally pagan holidays. If that's true, why do we celebrate them?

A. Like most celebrations, religious holidays usually have a great deal of tradition associated with them. Denise grew up in a church that was based more on tradition than on the right heart motive and she had that same question. If she couldn't find it in the Bible, she thought you shouldn't celebrate the day. It seems that what the first church leaders originally had in mind was to keep certain events in the hearts and minds of the believers. Most people didn't read back then, and having an annual calendar with certain things celebrated at specific times was a way of keeping a memorial of them. It's exactly like what God did when he instituted the feasts that Israel observes every year.

Nothing in the New Testament suggests that the church should have a schedule of traditional holidays. The only thing close to it is the observance of communion; but it's not specified how often we should keep it or what elements we should use—only that we should do it in remembrance of Jesus. However, since we have a tendency to be religious in our practices, it is only natural that men in the church would begin to imitate Israel's feasts with New Testament events. No doubt it had a certain amount of natural wisdom; but, on the whole, it was a man-idea rather than a God-idea.

As far as Christmas is concerned, it isn't accurately specified in scripture *when* Jesus Christ was born. The date we celebrate as Christmas, December 25, originated several centuries after the fact when the Roman emperor Constantine, a convert to Christianity, made belief in Jesus the state religion of the Roman Empire.

As well-intentioned as Constantine might have been, this was one of the worst things that could have happened. On his word, all of the pagan temples instantly became churches, sacrifices to false gods immediately ceased, and the idols were thrown out of the temples. But it was a superficial change. In order to protect their positions, the people in the hierarchy of pagan worship adopted Christianity as a new profession of faith without having a corresponding heart change. A lot of things remained in place for years. For instance, the mitered hats the popes wear are not much different than the headgear worn by the priests in the pagan temple worship.

The pagan holidays, for the most part, simply became Christian ones. That is the origin of the Christmas holiday. The festival of Saturnalia was the pagan feast associated with the winter solstice. People exchanged gifts at that time. Perhaps the scriptural account of the wise men giving gifts to Jesus provided the rationale, but whatever the reason, the feast of Saturnalia was replaced with the celebration of the birth of Jesus. It's not wrong to celebrate that, but as we said, there is no scriptural evidence stating that Jesus was born in the winter. In fact, a lot of scholars, along with some common sense thinking, find it hard to put shepherds keeping watch in the fields at night in the wintertime.

Easter had its origin as the celebration of the resurrection of Jesus, and rightly so. But because there was a pagan holiday associated with the beginning of Spring, things having to do with fertility and rebirth—like decorated eggs—were also celebrated along with it. We don't know exactly how the rabbits got in there, but the main point is that man's stuff got stirred in with God's stuff.

But anybody who has a heart for God will worship him in spirit and truth (John 4:23), even though other things may be happening all around them. Denise remembers one Christmas after she was saved when she was singing Christmas carols at her mom's house. She said as she thought about the lyrics to *O Come All Ye Faithful,* she was blown away by the fact that for as long as she could remember, she had sung that same song and didn't even know what it meant. Imagine all the people in the stores during the holiday season hearing these same songs with godly lyrics, and probably not even realizing that they are hearing the gospel. We can only hope that the truth in those words will come alive in their hearts as they listen.

Should we avoid these holidays since they are not "pure"? We don't think so. These holidays may be human in origin but the focus of our worship is genuine. It's an awesome thing that Jesus was born. We celebrate our own birthdays—how much more should we celebrate his? And if you can't get pumped about the resurrection of Jesus, maybe you need to get saved!!

Cremation   *Mark*

Q. My grandfather, who was a believer, was cremated. I've considered it for myself and my own father has also expressed this wish. Does this pose a problem for God in the resurrection? Is it a disgrace to the body? What is God's will concerning this?

A. Unfortunately, the Bible doesn't really say one way or another. It isn't even mentioned at all. You could maybe say that since cremation was not something that was done in the Bible, you shouldn't do it now. But, we can't say that it is unlawful to do it, or that it would affect our resurrected bodies, either. It does *not* change whether or not we are saved.

So, it is best to leave that question up to one's own conscience. It's not good to make rules where there are none.

Death and Sleep   *Mark*

Q. If people who die are not asleep until the resurrection, but are with the Lord in heaven, why are there references to sleeping and rest?

At thy rebuke, O God of Jacob, both the chariot and horse are cast into a dead sleep. (Psalm 76:6)

Consider and hear me, O LORD my God: lighten mine eyes, lest I sleep the sleep of *death.* (Psalm 13:3)

For this cause many are weak and sickly among you, and many sleep. (1 Corinthians 11:30)

Behold, I show you a mystery; We shall not all sleep, but we shall all be changed. (1 Corinthians 15:51)

A. Sleep was often used as a euphemistic term for death. You can tell that by the context of the way that it was used. For example, Jesus spoke of his friend Lazarus as *being asleep*. When the disciples said to him that if he was indeed sleeping then he would fine, the Lord told them plainly that Lazarus was dead. The Lord was using the word *sleep* to refer to the condition of the body which was dead and at rest. In other words, the body wasn't moving. Because Jesus knew what was going to happen, he also knew that wasn't a permanent condition for that body. The spirit of Lazarus was still in existence, waiting for Jesus' command to return to his body.

The verses we have listed all use the word *sleep*, but the meanings of that word are all different. In Psalm 76:6, the Hebrew word that means *dead sleep* could mean either sleep or death. The root of the word means "to stun or stupefy (with sleep or death)", as defined in *Strong's Concordance*. But in all six other instances of this word in the Old Testament, it means sleep, not death. In verse 5 of Psalm 76, when the scripture refers to men who have slept their sleep, both of those words mean sleep only.

In Psalm 13:3, when David says "lest I sleep the sleep of death", the word *sleep* means to be slack or languid and the word *death* means what it says. You'll notice in the *King James Version* that the words *sleep of* are italicized. These are words that the translators have put in to make the meaning more clear. You could accurately reword that last clause to say "lest I sleep in death" or "lest I die". So in this verse, David is talking about death.

Regarding the references given from 1 Corinthians, the context of the verses show that they both mean death, even though the true meaning of the Greek word used means "to put to sleep".

On the whole, the best way to interpret words like *sleep*, or any other words for that matter, is to view them in the context of the passage in which they are used. If we begin to try to define words with an idea that there is a secret meaning somewhere, we can get confused.

Desires Of The Heart   *Denise*

> *Delight thyself also in the LORD; and he shall give thee the desires of thine heart. Commit thy way unto the LORD; trust also in him; and he shall bring it to pass.* (Psalm 37:4-5)

In the book of Revelation, four times it is stated that God is the Alpha and the Omega, the beginning and the ending, the first and the last. The Holy Ghost showed me that as the Alpha, God is the one who *initiates* those godly desires in our hearts. The word "give" in verse 4 means to "ordain" or "assign". So when we think *we've* come up with a good or godly idea, we really shouldn't flatter ourselves. We received it from *God.* These desires are not haphazard ideas—they are God's own desires or assignments for our lives.

Now as the Omega, God brings these godly desires to pass in our life. Psalm 145:19 says, "He will fulfil the desire of them that fear him." In Matthew 5:17, Jesus said he did not come to destroy the law, but to fulfil it. In both of these verses, the word "fulfil" has similar meanings—*to accomplish, bring forth* or *execute.* Just as Jesus came to be the *executor* of his Father's will, we should do the same. The last part of Psalm 145:19 says, "of them that fear him". So this verse doesn't really apply to those who are outside of God's covenant, but to his children, who reverence him and follow his word.

We find God's will in his word, and Matthew 6:33 is a good place to start. "But seek ye first the kingdom of God, and his righteousness; and all these things shall be added unto you." This does not say to seek after the things, or the perfect ministry, but to seek *first* his king-dom. I like to combine this with Romans 12:2,

> And be not conformed to this world: but be ye transformed by the renewing of your mind, that ye may prove what is that good, and acceptable, and perfect, will of God.

This verse is instructing us to renew our minds—to line up our thinking with the word of God—so we can demonstrate his perfect will for our lives. I don't know about you, but it seems that the ideal thing would be to have God's will be done in my life, rather than my own will.

God does not dangle his desires in front of you like a carrot on the end of a stick, and tease you with them, knowing you will never be able to get to that carrot. He's the one who places *his* own desires on the inside of you, so they become *your* desires. Then he provides a way for you to achieve those desires. Philippians 1:6 in the *Amplified Bible* reads,

> And I am convinced and sure of this very thing,
> that He Who began a good work in you will continue
> until the day of Jesus Christ [right up to the time
> of His return], developing [that good work] and
> perfecting and bringing it to full completion in you.

The best thing Mark likes about the above verse is that it shows that the one who both starts and finishes the work is God, which takes the pressure off of us. And we're going to like the way we turn out because it's God who's doing it!

Did Jesus Go To Hell?   *Mark*

This is a big, big question. Depending on how you answer this, some people will say all manner of things about you. So I won't beat around the bush here. I think that Jesus did suffer in hell.

Now that's a mouthful, and since it has become a kind of litmus test for the "heretic hunters", this view really needs some explanation. I personally don't feel it's a heretical position. The reason that this upsets some segments of the body of Christ is because (this is how I've heard it expressed), "It is impossible for the nature of God to become the nature of Satan". It has been said that since man took on the nature of the devil when Adam fell, that if Jesus took on the nature of fallen man, he became like the devil.

That sounds logical, but I'm not sure I see it in those terms. I will say that people have pondered the nature of God, the devil, and of sin probably since Adam got kicked out of the garden. Scholars have written volumes about these subjects. So I'll just offer what may seem like a real simple perspective about the nature of God, the devil and mankind: we're self-centered, God is not. Every bit of evil, hatred, strife, lust, theft, murder, etc. comes from the root of selfishness. *Me, me, me.* Satan's fall was a result of the same thing.

It wasn't because God was self-centered that he sent Jesus to redeem us; and Jesus didn't go to the cross because he was looking for self-exaltation. Even in the crucifixion and death of Jesus, I don't believe there was a trace of sinfulness in him, not one bit. But I also have to believe the Bible when it says in 2 Corinthians 5:21 that *Jesus became sin.* I don't understand how that happened, but that's what it says. It doesn't say that he became like the devil; it says *he became sin. For us.* So we could become the righteousness of God in him.

We've talked with several people who said that *becoming sin* meant that Jesus put on sin like a coat and that he laid it off when he was resurrected. One problem with that perspective is that if Jesus was only *clothed* with sin, then we are only *clothed* with righteousness; we didn't really become righteous. The Bible is a spiritual book, but it's also logical. Here's the point: *Jesus became what we are, so we could become what he is. He suffered what we should have, so that we wouldn't get what we deserved.*

Another objection to the idea that Jesus went to hell is the idea that he became spiritually dead. How is it conceivable that God could be spiritually dead? Again, that idea doesn't give me fits like it does other people. The reason is because spiritual death simply means separation from God. As we know, once a person's physical body dies, it does not mean they cease to exist. Their spirit will either be with God, or be separated from God. If you look at Jesus on the cross when he asks, "My God, my God, why have you forsaken me?", it seems reasonable to assume, at that moment at least, that God had separated himself from Jesus because he had become sin. Using the definition of spiritual death that we just outlined, you could say that Jesus was spiritually dead. If separation from God was our punishment, then Jesus suffered to the fullest so that we wouldn't have to.

Maybe one reason this debate hasn't posed such a theological problem for me is that when I was a young Christian, I was reading through Psalm 18, one of David's songs. As most readers will know, a lot of the psalms are prophetic in the sense that they reveal events and doctrinal truths about Christ's life. For example, Psalm 22 is widely recognized to be describing Jesus on the cross from his point of view. But in Psalm 18:4-16, there is a first-person account of someone being delivered from hell by God himself in an awesome display of power and authority. When I read these verses, I knew just as surely as I know I'm saved, that this wasn't just an event in David's life; this was Jesus being raised from the dead. "He sent from above, he took me, he drew me out of many waters." (Psa 18:16) To this day, when I read this passage, it still gets all over me.

I freely admit I don't understand everything about this. I'm not sure that I need to, but I do understand this: because Jesus went through it, we won't have to. Praise God.

Did The Israelites Eat Steak? *Mark*

We were asked a question once about the animals that the Israelites had with them in the desert. Scripture says that God fed them with manna. However, it doesn't say anything about the people eating their animals, even though they were used in sacrifices. Why is that?

It's an interesting question and we aren't real sure we can give an adequate answer to this. Perhaps it's because the total amount of people that went out from Egypt has been estimated at between two and three million people. The meat requirements for a group that size would obviously be very large. It is stated in Exodus that they left Egypt with a great deal of animals but no number was given (Exod 12:38). We also don't know if they were accustomed to raising animals for food, at least, probably not in their function as slaves in Egypt. Some of the larger animals in cultures around the world are viewed primarily as work animals instead of as a source of food. We do know that they had enough animals to perform the sacrifices the Lord instituted while they were out in the desert.

Another thing to keep in mind is that in a desert environment, there is not much for animals to graze on. For example, Denise's cousin who raises cattle told us that in the state of Arizona, one cow needs 500 acres of grazing land to survive. With that in mind, if you think about a group of 2.5 million people in a desert for forty years, there really isn't an abundance of land that is going to produce a large herd of edible animals. That's our best guess as to why they didn't eat their livestock.

Esau's Blessing *Mark*

In Genesis 27, we have the account of Jacob conspiring with his mother Rebekah to deceive his father Isaac into giving him the blessing reserved for the firstborn son Esau. After Jacob was blessed by Isaac, Esau came in and found out about it. He asked Isaac if he had one blessing left for him.

> And Esau said unto his father, Hast thou but one blessing, my father? bless me, even me also, O my father. And Esau lifted up his voice, and wept. And Isaac his father answered and said unto him, Behold, thy dwelling shall be the fatness of the earth, and of the dew of heaven from above; And by thy sword shalt thou live, and shalt serve thy brother; and it shall come to pass when thou shalt have the dominion, that thou shalt break his yoke from off thy neck. (Gen 27:38-40)

Now, because of the circumstances surrounding this, and the fact that Jacob got better words spoken over him, people have drawn the conclusion that Esau was cursed. But if you look at these verses, it's not really a curse. It says that Esau would live of the fatness of the earth. That's actually a better deal than what God said to Adam about the ground being cursed and thorns and thistles coming forth (Gen 3:17-19). The phrase about serving his brother is not necessarily a curse, either. If you follow Esau's life, you find out that he actually did have a great number of riches, servants and herds, and eventually his descendants became the nation of Edom, which was conquered as Israel was passing through to the promised land. Edom finally disappeared from history because they always opposed the nation of Israel. That was not because they were cursed, but rather because of the choices they made.

The major thing to notice in this account is that Isaac actually did have the power to bless both Jacob and Esau, and the words of Isaac's mouth came to pass in their lives. The application of this passage is that there is also power in the words that we speak. If Isaac, who was not born again, had the power to bless his children, how much more do we as Christians have the power to bless our children with words of life and peace? Not only that, but we also should be taking every opportunity to speak words of life in every situation in which we find ourselves.

Fasting And Unbelief   *Denise*

Then came the disciples to Jesus apart, and said,
Why could not we cast him out? And Jesus said
unto them, Because of your unbelief: for verily I
say unto you, If ye have faith as a grain of mustard
seed, ye shall say unto this mountain, Remove
hence to yonder place; and it shall remove; and
nothing shall be impossible unto you. Howbeit
this kind goeth not out but by prayer and fasting.
(Matthew 17:19-21)

And he said unto them, This kind can come forth
by nothing, but by prayer and fasting.
(Mark 9:29)

(emphasis added)

You've probably read or heard the story about the
healing of the demoniac boy as told in the books of
Matthew, Mark and Luke. The boy, who had a dumb
spirit, would foam at the mouth, gnash his teeth, and
"falleth into the fire, and oft into the water" (Matt 17:15).
The boy's father sought out the disciples who had been
doing miracles in the name of Jesus, and "they could not
cure him" (v16). So the father begged Jesus to have com-
passion and help them. Jesus' reply was that if the father
could *believe*, then all things would be possible if he
believed. The father's response was that he did *believe*,
but he needed help getting rid of the *unbelief.*

In both Matthew and Mark, Jesus is recorded as saying
this kind goes out only by prayer and fasting. The "kind"
that is referred to in these passages is a kind of unbelief.
A great number of people we have spoken to, however,

have wrongly interpreted these scriptures saying *this kind* refers to a demon instead of unbelief, thinking if they will fast and pray enough, God will somehow be moved into doing something about the situation. But looking back to the question the disciples posed to Jesus in verse 19 about why they could not cast out the demon, Jesus' reply was "because of your *unbelief*" (Matt 17:20).

The disciples allowed their physical senses to determine their level of unbelief. Here they *saw* the boy doing things that were not normal. They most likely *heard* strange noises coming from the boy as he thrashed about as well as *hearing* others (including the father) say the boy was a lunatic. Two of their physical senses (sight and hearing) were communicating a level of unbelief to the disciples that would only be minimized through prayer and fasting.

Fasting and praying are not greater than the name of Jesus and won't get rid of demons; but it will at least minimize or get rid of our unbelief. We already have the faith of God on the inside of us, but if our unbelief is a stronger victor in our minds, then our actions will follow. The disciples had a level of unbelief from their physical senses that canceled out the faith they had in the word of God. The reason why we fast and pray is to discipline our flesh and mind to be more sensitive to the leading of the Holy Spirit. Matthew 8:16 says Jesus cast out the spirits with his word. He didn't stop and say, "I need to take some time to fast and pray, so I can command these spirits to leave." Jesus spent much of his time praying and was always led by the Spirit. He knew the authority he had. The devils know what you believe and they are subject to the name of Jesus and his authority working through you.

Fear Not   *Denise*

How many of us have heard it said that God has written 365 scriptures to "Fear not" in the Bible so we'd have one scripture to meditate on for each day of the year? Now that number seemed too coincidental for me, so I set out on my personal word search and found some interesting facts. The word *fear* or some semblance of that word is listed over 767 times in the Bible, and it's not always written as a directive to *not fear*. The actual instruction to "Fear not" is used only 90 times in the Bible. When you add up all the other commands—to not be dismayed, not have dread, or not be afraid—it comes up to a whopping 160 times in the word of God. A far smaller number than the actual 365 times I've heard misquoted time and time again.

However, no matter what negative circumstances we are faced with, the word of God is still true. It only takes one "Fear not, just believe" to keep us on the right track. God didn't give us a spirit of fear anyway, so it's not something we should think about and hang onto. I've heard an acronym for F.E.A.R. to be "False Evidence that Appears Real". God is not the author of fear or falseness. *Fear is an emotion that is not from God.*

There are five instances where the angel of the Lord appeared, and told someone "Fear not" (Matt 1:20; 28:5; Luke 1:13; 1:30; 2:10). Romans 8:15 says, "For ye have not received the spirit of bondage again to fear; but ye have received the Spirit of adoption, whereby we cry, Abba, Father." Can you see that? *Fear is a spirit of slavery; we have received the Spirit of adoption instead!*

So if God has not handed out fear, why should we buy into that bill of goods? Get rid of it! It's not from him. Got a bad report from the doctor? Go to doctor Jesus—he says you're healed. Lost your job? Promotion comes from the Lord—he's got something better. Second Corinthians 10:17 says *we* are in charge of casting down imaginations, and every high thing that exalts itself against the knowledge of God. Cast down that wrong thinking and replace it with a God thought. "God has given us a spirit of power and of love, a calm and well-balanced mind, and discipline and self-control." (2 Tim 1:7, paraphrased) So when everything around you is screaming for you to be afraid, the choice is ultimately up to you. You can choose to be carnal which leads to death or choose to be spiritually minded which is life and peace (Rom 8:6). Don't let fear take it's toll on you—choose life!

Give God The Glory *Denise*

Did you ever wonder about the biblical instruction to "give God the glory"? How can you give God something that he already has all of; something he said he would not share with another? Sometimes we just need to take time to think about those "churchy" type of sayings. The only reasonable place it seems for us to get glory from to give

to God would be out of our own born-again spirits, where
the Father, Son and Holy Ghost all make their abode.
Colossians 1:19 and 2:9 say that in Jesus all the fulness of
the Godhead dwelt. Colossians 2:10 says we "are complete in him" and John 1:16 says that of his fulness we
have received.

"God is a Spirit: and they that worship him must worship him in spirit and in truth." (John 4:24) The Bible
says that God inhabits the praises of his people (Psa 22:3)
and in his presence is fulness of joy (Psa 16:11). What
we actually do when we praise and worship the Lord is
release his presence, his joy, his love, and his glory into
our midst to do those things that only he can do. When
he does that, he is glorifying himself in us and we are
giving him his glory by allowing him to do it.

The word "glorify" means to magnify, honour, and
worship. Jesus said in Matthew 5:16 to let our light shine
that others may see our good works so the Father would
be glorified. In John 12:28, he prayed that the Father
would glorify his name, to which the Father replied, "I
have both glorified it, and will glorify it again." Jesus said
in John 16:14 that the Father would glorify Jesus.

And we can't overlook the recorded prayer of Jesus to
the Father in John 17, especially verses 5 through 12.
Here Jesus prays for the Father to glorify him with the
glory he had before he walked on the face of the earth.
He had demonstrated the Father's will to mankind and
fulfilled his ministry. He makes it a point to say that man
clearly understood and believed that the Father sent him;
that all those that believe on him were his Father's, and
his Father's were his, and then strangely enough Jesus
says that he is glorified in us.

So how do we release that glory? By faith, by praise, by worship, by our works—these are just some demonstrations of our faith to let God's light shine and to glorify him.

So . . . in your life, give God the glory!!!

Healing Is Part Of The Atonement   *Denise*

Q. When I read in Isaiah 53 that "he bore our sins", how does that line up with a physical illness? I looked in other Bible versions and did not find it to read as a physical illness, but only as a spiritual condition of sin.

A. *Many people don't believe that Jesus' promises actually include physical healing.* They may believe that their sins have been forgiven, but have a misconception that somehow healing *and* forgiveness of sins were not equally taken care of by Jesus.

When I first got saved, I learned the verse that said by Jesus' stripes we *were* healed (1 Pet 2:24). But I just didn't have the right revelation of this fact. I was taught something along the lines of "calling down from heaven" the healing power of God, rather than releasing the power into our physical body through our born-again spirit.

I once attended a church service where my head was hurting so bad that it felt like my skull was in a vise. I was lying down on the pew rubbing my head while listening to the guest speaker, Mark Brazee. Wouldn't you know it that he started teaching how it was no harder for God to heal than it was for God to forgive sins. Now *that* caught my attention because I had never recalled hearing that before. My ears perked up as I continued to listen; a light bulb went on in my head, and the pain left! I was so excited that after the message I went up and told him I was healed. My unbelief in God's word had been preventing me from receiving my healing that had *already been* purchased by Jesus.

Looking at the Gospels, we can see that when Jesus was physically on this earth, it was easy for people to believe that God could heal. But when Jesus started ministering to these same folks about forgiving their sins, they were aghast at the thought. It seems that man's thinking over the past couple thousand years has shifted 180 degrees. Nowadays, it seems that people can more readily receive their forgiveness of sins; but many have a mental block when it comes to believing God can and *has* healed every one who will believe. We think it's easier to receive forgiveness of sins because you can't see what sin or forgiveness looks like. But because healing is tangible, and you usually either feel it or see it, it's harder on your brain.

As Mark says, if you could have seen how bad your spirit looked before you got saved, you never would have believed it could be done. Likewise, if you could see how good your born-again spirit looks, you'd never want to go sin. We need to get our hearts lined up with the word of

God, so we can believe what we read. Healing is God's will. We need to assure our hearts of this fact.

Let's look at the following verses with the *Strong's Concordance* definitions in Hebrew added for emphasis.

Isaiah 53:3: "He *(Jesus)* is despised and rejected of men; a man of sorrows, and acquainted with grief (*choliy* – malady, anxiety, calamity, disease sickness): and we hid as it were our faces from him; he was despised, and we esteemed him not. (Verse 4) Surely he hath borne our griefs (same Hebrew word here – *choliy*), and carried our sorrows: yet we did esteem him stricken, smitten (to strike, beat, make [slaughter], punish, slay, (give) stripes, wound) and afflicted."

Verse 5 says, "But he was wounded for our transgressions (*pesha* – rebellion, sin, trespass), he was bruised (*daka* – to crumble; beat to pieces, break, crush, destroy, humble, oppress, smite) for our iniquities:(*avon* – perversity, evil, fault, punishment (of) sin) the chastisement (*muwcar* – reproof, warning or instruction, correction, discipline,) of our peace (*shalowm* – safe, happy; welfare, i.e. health, prosperity) was upon him; and with his stripes (*chabbuwrah* – a weal (or black-and-blue mark)– bruise, hurt, wound.) we are healed (*rapha* – to mend (by stitching), cure, heal, physician, repair, make whole)."

Some might say that's in the Old Testament, so it doesn't apply to us today. Okay, what about the New Testament? Let's look at Matthew 8:17 with some Greek meanings from *Strong's*: "That it might be fulfilled which was spoken by Esaias the prophet, saying, Himself took (*lambano* – to get hold of; accept, attain, hold, obtain, receive) our infirmities (*astheneia* – feebleness (of body or mind); malady; frailty; disease, sickness, weakness), and bare (*bastazo* – to lift, endure, declare, sustain, receive, carry, take up) our sicknesses (*nosos* – a malady, disease, infirmity, sickness)."

In 1 Peter 2:24, we see the same truth: "Who his own self bare our sins in his own body on the tree, that we, being dead to sins, should live unto righteousness: by whose stripes (*molops* – a mole ("black eye") or blow, mark) ye were healed (*iaomai* – to cure, heal, make whole)."

It's plain from scripture that if we *were* healed 2000 years ago through Jesus dying on the cross, then it is still a spiritual reality for today. It's all a matter of our understanding and believing the truth. Sickness may come to attack us, but in the spirit we are completely healed. Let's command our physical bodies to get in line with this truth. Take your responsibility to use God's authority in your life.

We realize the main problem God had with man was sin, and that the primary purpose of the Jesus' atoning sacrifice was to get rid of the sin nature in mankind. But sickness and disease are a result of the fallen nature of man and therefore were also included in the atonement. For other books about this subject, we encourage you to pick up F.F. Bosworth's, *The Healer.*

Hebrews 10:26 *Mark*

It seems almost inevitable that after a person gets saved, for one reason or another they fall into something stupid and end up committing sin. OK, maybe not you, but not everybody's perfect. Since that is true, a lot of preaching gets directed at our actions; a lot of people are feeling like they've "backslidden"; a lot of saved people are going down to the altar to get saved again. This situation is great for the devil, who will use your own sin to beat you up; and your own conscience, as well as a lot of Christians, will agree.

This has also led to the doctrine that says you can lose your salvation by sinning, a doctrine I like to call the "insecurity of the believer". And there are some verses in scripture that would seem to point in that direction.

I'm not going to get into a lengthy discussion about all of these, since it is beyond the scope of the format of this book; however, I feel the verse in Hebrews 10:26 needs to be clarified because a lot of people get tripped up on this one. It bothered me a lot when I first saw it, and I've also talked with many who have been troubled by this same verse as well. It says:

> For if we sin wilfully after that we have received the knowledge of the truth, there remaineth no more sacrifice for sins. (Heb 10:26)

This is talking about a saved person wilfully engaging in sin and losing their relationship with God, isn't it? I used to think so, until I got a better understanding of the nature of our salvation. It's not fragile, thank God!

Let's take a closer look. First of all, the word *if* is not in the original language. That's very important. This is not the kind of statement that is saying "If you do this, then this will happen". But, admittedly I'm no Greek scholar; I simply found this out by reading an interlinear New Testament that shows the Greek text with the English words underneath. This is the way the English words are ordered: *wilfully for sinning us after the to receive the full knowledge of the truth, no more concerning sins remains a sacrifice.* That may seem a little unclear (!?), but there definitely is no *if.*

Really, the only way to figure it out is by looking at the surrounding verses. The context of this passage in chapter 10 is about the perfect sacrifice of Jesus for *all* sin. The writer was addressing this to Jews who were much more familiar with the system of sacrifices that had been in place for centuries than they were with the final offering for all sin forever. He was saying, and the surrounding verses give the context, that if you persisted in your old way of dealing with your sin (by offering blood sacrifices according to the law of Moses), after having received Jesus as your savior, there was no more sacrifice for you. If you do that you will have counted the blood of Jesus as nothing and essentially spit in the face of God's grace.

The key to this interpretation lies in verse 14, "For by one offering he hath perfected for ever them that are sanctified", and verse 18 which says, "Now where remission of these is, there is no more offering for sin." *What is it that perfects us forever, if not the offering of Jesus?* After we have been made clean, does our salvation then depend on us staying sinless? If we maintain the position that it is now up to us to stay saved by our works, then what we're really saying is that the blood of Jesus' sacrifice is not any better than the sacrifice of an animal. We are counting the blood of Jesus right down there with the blood of bulls and goats. What an amazing insult! This is the sin that the writer is describing in verse 26. Like he says, let us hold fast to the profession of our faith in the awesome power of Jesus' blood.

A lot more could be said about this subject, but the conclusion that you've lost your salvation if you sin wilfully is totally wrong. None of us could remain saved if that were true. Think about it—there aren't a whole lot of sins that aren't wilful. Sin occurs when we give our own will more value than God's will.

In Romans 6:2 it says that we are dead to sin, seeing that we have been baptized into his death. Since we are dead in Christ, we are free from sin (v7); in other words, we are free from sin's effects. This is the whole point of Paul's epistle to the Galatians, i.e., "Are we so stupid that we think that after receiving the Spirit by faith, we have to be perfected or completed by keeping the law?" (Gal 3:3) We couldn't do it before Jesus; we can't do it now (Acts 15:5 with verses 10-11). Sin has consequences that are lasting and unpleasant, but God no longer relates to us based on what we do. He looks at us based on what Jesus has done. Praise God!

Hedge Of Protection – Not!   *Denise*

Q. Is praying a hedge of thorns for protection around a person biblical?

A. In the Old Testament, it was common for people to pray to God to build a hedge around a person for protection, but hopefully they were thinking that the thorns might be on the outside rather than on the inside of the hedge! You will never read in the New Testament that Jesus, or anyone else, prayed for a hedge of thorns. There are only two places where we see the phrase "hedge of thorns" in the Bible. One is in Proverbs 15:19 (emphasis added): "The way of the slothful man is as a *hedge of thorns:* but the way of the righteous is made plain." The other is in Hosea 2:6 (emphasis added): "Therefore, behold, I will *hedge up thy way with thorns,* and make a wall, that she shall not find her paths." *The words hedge and protection do not appear together anywhere in the Bible!*

As Jesus was praying for the disciples and the church in John 17, he prayed not that his Father would take us out of the world, but that he would keep us from evil. This lines up with scripture in Psalm 23 that God has prepared a table for us in the presence of our enemies. We are here for the long haul. Paul wrote, "And the Lord shall deliver me from every evil work, and will preserve me unto his heavenly kingdom." (2 Tim 4:18)

When we understand our position of authority as New Testament believers, protection from the world is not a primary concern. Let's use courage and boldness to go out into the world and change lives and circumstances with the power that resides in us. Jesus wasn't walking around in fear and trembling, but he was walking around like his dad owned the place . . . and he still does!

Jesus As Our Intercessor   *Mark*

> *Wherefore he is able also to save them to the uttermost that come unto God by him, seeing he ever liveth to make intercession for them.*
> (Hebrews 7:25)

> *At that day ye shall ask in my name: and I say not unto you, that I will pray the Father for you*
> (John 16:26)

Q. According to John 16, Jesus is not acting as High Priest in the traditional Jewish manner, i.e., we pray in Jesus' name and he goes to the Father but rather our prayers, in Jesus' name, take us directly to the throne of God. So what does Hebrews 7:25 mean?

A. The role of a priest always has been as an intermediary between God and man—to act as man's representative before God, and God's representative before man. Obviously, the role of Jesus as our high priest is on a higher level than any other priest because he is both God and man.

But look at Hebrews 8:3: "For every high priest is ordained to offer gifts and sacrifices . . ." This means that the high priest did not, as a primary function, plead with God or make requests. This may run contrary to the current emphasis on intercessory prayer. The high priest's main duty was to handle the various sacrificial rituals and offerings having to do with sin, the Day of Atonement, and so forth. That is a true intercessory, intermediary role.

So Jesus as high priest offered himself as the one sacrifice for sins forever. He was then raised from the dead and is currently seated on the right hand of God. Every time the Father looks at Jesus he sees the eternal sacrifice made on behalf of our sin, and also the eternal "intercessor" who offered it. We could accurately paraphrase Hebrews 7:25 like this, "Jesus lives forever as one who not only was the intercessor, but also the everlasting sacrifice, and because of his unchangeable position as priest is able to save completely them that come to him."

It's for that reason that the way to the Father is open, and that is why the statement Jesus made in John 16:26 is true.

Jezebel Spirit   *Denise*

There have been so many teachings about so many things, just because it "tickles the ear" or may make someone a lot of money. And it's sad that Christians are going around trying to "play" the Holy Ghost, instead of *listening* to what he's telling us. When Mark and I were in a tent meeting in the UK about 10 years ago, there was a woman who was demonized. How do we know that? Well, she was on the dirt floor of the tent on her hands and knees, clawing the air and you could plainly see she was being tormented. Mark went over by her to check it out, and he heard people praying for her trying to cast out different spirits. One man was even trying to cast out a "spirit of Jezebel". *Now where does the Bible say there is a Jezebel spirit?* Nowhere.

This woman was sort of pushing the other people away from her saying that they didn't know how to pray, and she said to Mark, "But you, . . ." as she pointed right at him. Well, he took that as his "green light" that he was on the right track. Mark stood behind her and started praying in tongues to get direction from the Holy Ghost, and he heard God say this woman was terrified; so he spoke to that spirit of fear and terror and commanded it out of her. The moment he did that, the demon left and the woman collapsed on the ground. When she stood up, her countenance had been transformed from fear to peace.

So the next time you may want to say someone has a Jezebel spirit, think again. Don't confuse what you may observe with your physical senses with what you actually hear from the Holy Spirit. If you look at the story of

Jezebel, she was really a controlling woman who provoked and persuaded her husband, and she wound up going to the dogs.

> But there was none like unto Ahab, which did
> sell himself to work wickedness in the sight of
> the LORD, whom Jezebel his wife stirred up.
> (1 Kings 21:25)

Judgment As A Motivator   *Mark & Denise*

One thing we would like to take issue with is the idea that we need to preach the judgment of God as a motivation for people to come to God. The Bible says in Romans that it is the goodness of God—not his anger—that leads man to repentance. People have heard the judgment and wrath of God preached from the pulpit for centuries, and it has not brought the world any closer to God.

In Luke 2:14, the heavenly host praised God saying, "Glory to God in the highest, and on earth peace, good will toward men." This does not say that men are at peace with men, but rather that God's peace and good will is toward men—not God's wrath.

For this is as the waters of Noah unto me: for as I
have sworn that the waters of Noah should no more
go over the earth; *so have I sworn that I would not be
wroth with thee*, nor rebuke thee. For the moun-
tains shall depart, and the hills be removed; but my
kindness shall not depart from thee, *neither shall the
covenant of my peace be removed,* saith the LORD
that hath mercy on thee. (Isa 54:9-10; emphasis
added)

In the above verses, God swears an oath that he would
not be wroth with us and that the covenant of his peace,
his binding word, would not be removed. Knowing that
God is not mad at us makes all the difference in how we
perceive him. Jesus' death on the cross was payment for
all our sins—past, present and future. No matter how
many times we miss it, we can still understand that he is
not angry with us. To quote Arthur Meintjes, "Even if
you were to walk outside and see it raining down fire and
brimstone, you need to know it's not God judging you."

When a person understands that the Supreme Being
in all the universe loves them personally, regardless of the
sin in their lives, and has in fact, already paid the penalty
for that sin, that's when you see hearts start to change.
That's when people start to come towards God instead of
staying away from him.

Love is the most attractive thing in the universe. We
agree that there is a coming judgment, and wrath will be
poured out on the world at some point; but we preach the
gospel of God from the point of his grace, his love, and
his mercy. We have found that to be an effective way to
communicate the gospel to people, and we are in good
company. The apostle Paul's letters are full of God's

grace. That is what the church should be preaching to this lost and dying world.

Killing Or Murder – Heart Motive   *Mark*

Q. There seem to be apparent contradictions in Exodus 20:13 and Leviticus 24:17 compared to Exodus 32:27 and I Samuel 15:2,3,7,8. Can you explain?

A. Sometimes what looks like a contradiction isn't really that at all. The one about "thou shalt not kill" is all about the motive behind the act. If you take the commandment in a technical-to-the-letter sense then, of course, any killing would be sin and even God would be a sinner for commanding certain people to be put to death. And in the beginning of the earth, even those who killed (such as Cain) were given a pass on judgment. However, you should recognize that God himself set up capital punishment in Genesis 9:6. This occurred after the flood, which was in itself, the first example of capital punishment. Therefore the commandment against killing in Exodus 20:13, etc. is more logically interpreted as being a commandment against murder.

Remember that physical death is not what the Bible defines as death. In Genesis 2:17, God told Adam that in the day he would eat of the fruit, he would "surely die." If we take death to mean a ceasing of physical life, then God lied to Adam. No, death in this instance, and forever after, means loss of intimacy and relationship with God. So, when God ordered groups of people to be killed, he was most likely reckoning them to be already dead spiritually, and also beyond reach. Things were a lot different prior to the resurrection.

Mark Of The Beast *Mark*

When I got saved in 1979, I read through the book of Revelation for the first time in one night. It says in Revelation 1:3 that you are blessed if you read that book. So I was blessed, I'm sure, but I was also more than a little confused by most of what I read. Prior to getting saved, I took little notice of what was going on in the world. But, as time went on, and Israel got into a war with Lebanon, my eagerness to see Jesus sitting on the throne in Jerusalem led to a change in my perspective. I did begin to see that God does indeed have a "world view".

At that time, even as it is in these days, there was no lack of ministries that focused almost exclusively on how prophecy was being revealed in the newspapers and on TV every day. I couldn't help but notice that there were a lot of points of view that differed. In fact, the recently published *Spirit Filled Life Study Bible* outlines no less than five of the most common interpretations of the book of Revelation, as well as eight views of the rapture. Just from my own personal observation, the subject of end-time prophecy seems to bring the more hysterical, irrational segments of the body of Christ out into the open.

So let me acknowledge that I am not in any way an expert on this subject. By design. We don't—and probably won't ever—make end-time prophecy a real dominant focus in our ministry, partly because prophecy is so easy to misinterpret before it happens.

God does not reveal all his cards ahead of time. Jesus' first appearance here was prophesied, but yet most did not recognize him when he got here. Remember what Jesus said to the Pharisees, the guys who went over the word with a fine-tooth comb?

> Ye have not his word abiding in you: for whom he hath sent, him ye believe not. Search the scriptures; for in them ye think ye have eternal life: and they are they which testify of me. And ye will not come to me, that ye might have life. (John 5:38-40)

Here were these puffed up religious experts, wanting to kill the very source of the word they professed to believe. What that scripture tells me is that if I cling, white knuckled, to some kind of preconception about how the last days are going to play out, I could be wrong just as easily as these Pharisees were.

So what is the "mark of the beast" mentioned in Revelation 13:16-18? There is a lot of speculation about that mark, a lot of it having to do with the technology of the day. With all our financial and personal information becoming more digital on a year-by-year basis, you can understand how that might make some people nervous. But, I don't really know what it is—sorry, I can't give you anything substantive about that computer chip in the flesh.

However, one thing I absolutely do know is this: nobody is going to accidentally miss it. If you have a heart for God, he will save you. Our Father doesn't just trick us into going to hell. The best course of action is to stay close to him, stay focused on doing his will and you'll be alright. He's looking to get us across the finish line, not looking for a chance to disqualify us.

I also don't see any way around Israel's involvement in the last days. There are too many unfulfilled promises for them to be completely out of the picture. If you want to pray for the nation, pray for the peace of Jerusalem (Psa 122:6). They need it.

The most valuable skill you can ever learn is how to be sensitive to the spirit of God. Especially in these last days . . .

More Sure Word *Denise & Mark*

There's a section in the apostle Peter's second letter, first chapter, that we really like, particularly in these noisy days. He starts his thought by saying that he didn't follow *cunningly devised fables* but was an eyewitness of the power and coming of the Lord Jesus Christ. He goes on to say he *heard* God the Father's voice in a cloud of glory saying he was well pleased with his beloved Son. Peter was with Moses and Elijah when they were on the mountain *talking* with Jesus. Peter *saw* Jesus' face and clothes shine like the sun. Peter was an eyewitness, an onlooker, to Jesus' majesty. I don't know about you, but I'm guessing this would have made a lasting impression.

To paraphrase what Peter said, "We have also a *more sure word* (set in concrete)of prophecy, and it would be good if you'd fixate on it and pay attention to it, like you would pay attention to a light continually shining in a dark place, until daylight comes." What Peter is saying here is that God's word is more sure, more real, and more stable, than what he had seen with his own eyes. That's amazing! This is so contrary to how we normally act.

Have you ever heard the sayings, "I'll believe it, when I see it", or "Let's wait and see . . ."? More emphasis is placed on the observations made by our five physical senses than on the actual word of God. Romans 8:6 says, "For to be carnally minded is death; but to be spiritually minded is life and peace."

Peter was saying, "Look, we didn't make this stuff up, we saw it all as it happened, but you know what? The word of God is more real than that because it was his word that caused everything we saw." (Mark's para-phrase)

What does this mean to us? It means that no matter what our situation or experience is, God's promises are more real than what we can experience with our five senses. This is why Peter said you would do well to take heed to that word, like a light in a dark place, until day comes, until the light of the word rises up in your heart and overtakes your circumstances.

Moses And Zipporah   *Mark*

> *And it came to pass by the way in the inn, that the LORD met him* (Moses), *and sought to kill him. Then Zipporah took a sharp stone, and cut off the foreskin of her son, and cast it at his feet, and said, Surely a bloody husband art thou to me. So he let him go: then she said, A bloody husband thou art, because of the circumcision.* (Exodus 4:24-26)

Q. Did God want to kill Moses? If so, why?

A. The passage in Exodus 4:24-26 is one of the most obscure and difficult to understand scriptures in the word of God. I remember when I first read this, I had no idea what was going on. There are a couple of different ways you could look at it and there are a couple of different things involved.

One factor is that God's covenant with Abraham and his descendants at that point of time required circumcision as an identifying mark of the covenant. God told Abraham in Genesis 17:10 and 17:14:

> This is my covenant, which ye shall keep, between me and you and thy seed after thee (v10); Every man child among you shall be circumcised. And the uncircumcised man child whose flesh of his foreskin is not circumcised, that soul shall be cut off from his people; he hath broken my covenant (v14).

Zipporah, Moses' wife, was a Midianite and therefore was a stranger to that covenant, and it seems from this passage that Moses and Zipporah had differences where this is concerned. It is probable that Zipporah was the one against the circumcision and Moses went along with her.

However, God demanded this circumcision take place or there were going to be serious consequences. One key to understanding this passage lies in applying verse 23 in this chapter as something that God said to Moses, instead of Pharoah: "And I say unto thee, let my son go, that he may serve me: and if thou refuse to let him go, behold, I will slay thy son, even thy firstborn." In other words, God was saying: *Moses, if you don't send forth Gershom to serve me* (by way of circumcision), *then I will kill him.* Therefore, God was seeking to kill Gershom in verse 24, not Moses.

Before we accuse God of being unjust, we need to realize that God had a very important task for Moses to do. God was about to give the law to the nation of Israel through Moses. Therefore it was required that Moses keep those ordinances that were to be established. After all, the lawgiver ought to be keeping the same law that he gives.

Maybe you can ask Moses about it yourself when you get to heaven (smile). At any rate, circumcision is not something that is a law today. God is not going to place any judgment on us regarding the commandment of circumcision because we are not under the law anymore. And also because he has already placed all judgment on Jesus. That's why it's important for us to believe and receive what Jesus has done for us.

Nailed, Not Tied   *Mark*

Q. Why did they nail Jesus to the cross instead of tying him to the cross like the others?

A. Nailing a person's hands and feet to the cross was a typical method of crucifixion. There is no verse in scripture that would tell us the thieves were tied to the cross while Jesus was nailed to the cross. Punishment in the

Roman empire took many forms, and crucifixion was a punishment that was done differently at different times and for different offenses. For example, tradition records that Peter was crucified upside down.

However, there is a prophecy in the Old Testament in Psalm 22:16 which says, ". . . they pierced my hands and my feet." So even though the scripture doesn't say specifically that Jesus was nailed to the cross, we believe that he was. This is an example of circumstances coming together in such a way that prophecy was being fulfilled, even in the method of crucifixion.

There are many other references in Psalm 22 to the crucifixion. One could read the entire psalm from Jesus' point of view on being crucified. That is instructive as to what he went through.

Again, there is no scriptural evidence to suggest that the two thieves were tied instead of nailed. They were still alive after Jesus died, and it is recorded that the Roman soldiers came and broke the legs of the two thieves so that the internal pressure of hanging from the cross would kill them quickly. This was at the request of the Jewish rulers who didn't want the Passover to be defiled by the sight of dead people on the outskirts of the city. Ordinarily, someone who was crucified could endure for about two to three days. According to *Unger's Bible Dictionary*, there was an instance recorded of someone enduring crucifixion for nine days before they died.

It was extremely unlikely that someone would die from being crucified in a period of just six hours. So even Jesus' death was supernatural. He was in control of every aspect of the situation, even to the moment that he gave up the ghost. As he himself said in John 10:17-18: "I lay down my life, that I might take it again. No man taketh it from me, but I lay it down of myself. I have power to lay it down, and I have power to take it again."

No Condemnation   *Mark & Denise*

> *There is therefore now no condemnation to them which are in Christ Jesus, who walk not after the flesh, but after the Spirit. (Romans 8:1)*

Q. If Romans 8:1 says there is no condemnation, then why do I feel bad when I do something wrong?

A. As you follow God's word—not just hearing it but doing it—you are following the leading of the Spirit, where there is no condemnation. However, if you choose to follow after your own flesh instead of the spirit, you can pretty much be assured you'll get into condemnation by way of your own conscience.

You have to continually keep your focus on the truth of God's love. 1 John 3:19 says, "We love him, because he *first* loved us." That verse was there before you ever sinned, and it's there after you sin. It's even there while you're sinning. Why are we saying this? Because the condemnation that you feel is not coming from God. It's coming from either the devil or your own conscience. It really doesn't matter where it comes from; it's still wrong. God will never condemn you, even while you are in the midst of sinning.

Does that mean that we should continue in sin? Like the scripture says, "God forbid." Well, why not? If God's already put our sin on Jesus, and won't judge us, why not just go ahead and let the grace of God abound and let it get a real good workout in our lives? What's the reason we shouldn't give in to sin, if it doesn't matter?

The reason is that when we sin, we feel condemned. When our hearts condemn us, we lose our confidence before God. We start taking our eyes off him, and start focusing on our own inadequacies and shortcomings, forgetting that, as believers, we look just like Jesus in our spirits. We open up the door to the accuser, the devil, and he'll take every opportunity we give him to destroy our confidence.

Scripture says in 1 John 3:18-19 that if we love in deed and in truth, we assure our hearts before God. Verse 20 says that if our heart condemns us, God is greater than our heart and knows all things. This means that though your own heart or conscience may give you a hard time, God *will not* because he is greater than your heart. He knows our true nature, the new creature that he has made us to be, who we are in the spirit.

Verse 21 continues with, "Beloved, if our heart condemn us not, then have we confidence toward God." The reverse of that statement is also true—if our heart does condemn us, then we don't have confidence before God. Since everything in our relationship with God is accessed by our faith, our confidence is very important. The reason that sin is so deadly for a believer, is that it affects the conscience of a believer. If that conscience is condemning you, you will have a hard time believing that God is going to do anything for you.

It's actually good to know that we have a sensitive conscience, but it never feels good when it's defiled. Thankfully, the things that we see with our eyes or do with our bodies do not affect the new birth that has taken place in our spirit.

Our salvation is independent of our actions. Acts of righteousness do not cause us to be saved. Acts of sin do not cause us to lose our salvation. However, sin does open us up to the condemnation that the devil brings to our mind. It's not without reason that he is called the *accuser of the brethren.*

Onan's Problem   *Mark*

The subject of birth control isn't specifically addressed in scripture and that's probably why most preachers don't comment on it much. Some, however, have said that because God slew Onan for not giving his seed to his brother's wife, it is sinful to engage in sex for any other reason than reproduction. But to jump from the example of Onan and his punishment to that conclusion is a leap that seems way too far.

Let's take a look and see what really went on.

And Judah took a wife for Er his firstborn, whose name was Tamar. And Er, Judah's firstborn, was wicked in the sight of the LORD; and the LORD slew him. And Judah said unto Onan, Go in unto thy brother's wife, and marry her, and raise up seed to thy brother. And Onan knew that the seed should not be his; and it came to pass, when he went in unto his brother's wife, that he spilled it on the ground, lest that he should give seed to his brother. And the thing which he did displeased the LORD: wherefore he slew him also.
(Genesis 38:6-10)

Lots of people have used this passage to teach against masturbation or contraception, but that isn't the point at all. This was simply the refusal on Onan's part to obey his father in carrying on the lineage of Judah through the firstborn son Er's wife. It displayed a real wicked attitude on Onan's part in selfishly wanting Er's inheritance. We can't be 100% sure, but Onan probably wanted to place himself in the position of the firstborn son. If Tamar had a child through Onan, the inheritance would have bypassed Onan and gone directly to his child.

As far as the will of God goes in controlling the size of our families, it seems as though that part of it falls under our own control. Abortion as a means of birth control is clearly wrong, but prevention of conception isn't really addressed. That being the case, we should follow the peace of God about it (Col 3:15).

Playing With The Occult   *Denise*

People all over the world are seeking the supernatural, but most are looking for it on the wrong side of the cross. After all, they wonder, what could really be the harm? Certainly you're not selling your soul to the devil and nothing bad could possibly happen to you—or could it? Growing up, the kids around my street would have fun creating makeshift "haunted houses" where, for a small fee, you could be blindfolded and led through a maze of rooms and not only have the hair on the back of your neck stand up and feel the adrenaline rush of fear in the pit of your stomach, but put your hands on "brains" (cold spaghetti noodles), feel "eyeballs" (peeled grapes), and hear chains rattle.

While mom would get up in the mornings and go for the daily crossword puzzle, I'd read our daily horoscope (since we were the same "sign"), so we would know what to expect from the day—good or bad. Even at the Catholic grade school I attended, I played a British witch in the school play. And who could forget the Christmas shows where we sang the Age of Aquarius? Several of my family members, including myself, even went to psychics to see what the future would bring. We played the *Ouija* board game, *Kreskin's ESP*, and even the *Magic 8 Ball*. After all, it was so mysterious and fun. I even remember seeing hypnotists in the lounges as our evening entertainment. "So what's the big deal?" you ask.

After I got saved, I made it a point to try to get the answers to my questions from the Bible. In my heart, I believed it was truth (though I couldn't prove it then), and I had to correct my preconceived ideas and wrong thinking about God and man. Christian radio programs didn't really help me, and actually got me more confused than I already was. And there didn't seem to be many people who could give me clear cut scriptural to my questions. I didn't even know there was such a thing as a Christian bookstore! Imagine my surprise when I went back to the Catholic church I was brought up in and asked where I could purchase a *King James Bible*. You would have thought I asked for the plague . . . but that's another story.

One of the first things I did after accepting Jesus was to get rid of some board games I still had, including the *Ouija* board. A well-meaning neighbor had me tossing out just about everything in my place including records, cassettes, candlestick holders and third-world art; it seemed she spotted a "devil on every doorknob" in my house. Well, not wanting to displease God or my "well-educated" neighbor, I went along with it all. It wasn't until some time later, that I was able to see for myself what was truly ungodly or demonic.

I discovered that fortune telling, tarot cards, astrology, psychics, etc., all fall into the category of witchcraft. Witchcraft is defined as (1) the use of sorcery or magic; (2) communication with the devil or with a familiar; (3) an irresistible influence or fascination: enchantment (*Webster's Ninth New Collegiate Dictionary*). On the surface, none of the things I did seemed really that bad, but Deuteronomy 18:10-12 says,

> There shall not be found among you any one that maketh his son or his daughter to pass through the fire, or that useth divination, or an observer of times, or an enchanter, or a witch, Or a charmer, or a consulter with familiar spirits, or a wizard, or a necromancer. *For all that do these things are an abomination unto the LORD:* and because of these abominations the LORD thy God doth drive them out from before thee. (emphasis added)

2 Kings 17:17 says,

> And they caused their sons and their daughters to pass through the fire, and used divination and enchantments, and sold themselves to do evil in the sight of the LORD, to provoke him to anger.

And Jeremiah 27:9 says,

> Therefore hearken not ye to your prophets, nor to your diviners, nor to your dreamers, nor to your enchanters, nor to your sorcerers, which

speak unto you, . . .

The bottom line is that witchcraft is a work of the flesh (Gal 5:20)—there's nothing spiritual about it, and there's nothing to be afraid of either. Does that make it right? No. But it's not a godly thing. It doesn't have any more or less power than wrath or envy.

God is a supernatural being, so we have a desire for the supernatural. As Christians we've been given his authority with the name of Jesus to demonstrate and see the supernatural power of God through signs and wonders in our lives and the lives of others. What more could you want? We need to seek the supernatural on the right side of the cross.

Praying For The Lost   *Mark*

How should we effectively pray for lost people? Especially in light of the fact that God won't counteract a person's own will, even to save them from hell. Even more, how are we supposed to pray in faith, seeing that there is no guarantee that anyone will accept Jesus as their savior?

Many people think that if they pray hard enough, then surely God is obligated to answer their prayer and save that person. The fact is, God has already obligated himself to save anyone who comes to the Lord for salvation. The real issue lies in getting them to come, and there are some things we can and should pray for regarding that.

When you pray for a lost person, you need to pray for someone to come across their path who knows God, knows his love, and his word; and can speak it into their life. "Pray ye therefore the Lord of the harvest, that he will send forth labourers into his harvest." (Matt 9:38) If the way is open, don't be surprised if he sends you. Let God's word do its own work. Remember, it's not our prayer that saves; it is the word of God and a person's response to it. Faith comes by hearing the word, so that is the primary need. As it says in Romans 10:14-15:

> . . . how shall they believe in him of whom they
> have not heard? and how shall they hear without
> a preacher? And how shall they preach, except
> they be sent?

The Holy Ghost will take the word and minister understanding and faith concerning the need for Jesus, and also concerning Jesus' love. The only sin that sends anyone to hell is the sin of unbelief—not believing in Jesus. "And when he is come, he will reprove the world of sin, . . . , Of sin, because they believe not on me." (John 16:8-9) That's something the Holy Ghost will do without you having to pray for it, but he still needs to use the word of God.

Remember to also use the authority of the name of Jesus to command the devil to take his hands off of that person's spiritual eyesight. 2 Corinthians 4:4 says, ". . . the god of this world hath blinded the minds of them which believe not, lest the light of the glorious gospel of Christ, who is the image of God, should shine unto them." This is something you can pray more or less on a daily basis, because an unsaved person doesn't always know any better than to keep on opening up the door to the devil through their words or actions.

Another very effective way to pray for unsaved people is taken from Ephesians 1:17-19, and you can personalize it for particular people:

> That the God of our Lord Jesus Christ, the Father of glory, may give unto you the spirit of wisdom and revelation in the knowledge of him: The eyes of your understanding being enlightened; that ye may know what is the hope of his calling, and what the riches of the glory of his inheritance in the saints, And what is the exceeding greatness of his power to us-ward who believe, according to the working of his mighty power, Which he wrought in Christ, when he raised him from the dead, and set him at his own right hand in the heavenly places.

Keep in mind that God is more eager than we are to see people get saved, so you don't have to beg and plead with God for this to be important to him. This is what he's after, and he's already on it.

Preserve Us   *Denise*

Have you ever wondered why God doesn't just zap us out of difficult situations? We have. What's even more disturbing is that we are promised in Psalm 23 that God would prepare a table before us in the *presence* of our enemies. That means our enemies are still going to be around us. *Satan was even present with Jesus at the last supper.* Think about it!

In searching the scriptures, I discovered that although God never promised us that we would be taken out of the world, he did promise that he would keep us (preserve) from evil (John 17:15). In 2 Timothy 4:18, the Greek word for *preserve* is *sozo*, meaning to save, deliver, and protect. In Old Testament scriptures, various definitions of *preserve* are given in Hebrew including "to reserve, save and regard". Throughout Psalms we see the word *preserve* over and over, whether in prayers *to* the Lord, or in promises *from* him. Psalm 145:20 says, "The Lord preserveth all them that love him." God says he would preserve the simple, the faithful, the saints, man and beast; preserve us from trouble, and preserve our life.

As I was listening to the Holy Ghost, he pointed out to me that my favorite jelly growing up was strawberry preserves. The picture he gave me was this: If a jar of jelly sits on the shelf in a store for a long time, no matter how much dust or dirt gathers around it, or if it gets splashed from someone cleaning the floors, the contents of the jar remain preserved or protected because of the seal on the jar. Even after you get the jelly home, you can count on it being just as fresh when you open it as when it was made.

Both Ephesians 2:13 and 4:30 say we are *sealed* with
the holy Spirit of promise. So just like that jar of jelly,
our spirit is also sealed, but with the promises of God.
No matter how much dirt we may get into, we still have
God's guarantee. He will preserve us in every situation
because we have the overcomer living on the inside of us.
Greater is he that is in me than he that is in the world
(1 John 4:4).

Real Versus Counterfeit   *Denise*

In order to be able to speak out about Christianity,
you need to study the real thing—not the counterfeits.
I'm sure all of us at one time or another have either
known someone or met up with people whose friends or
family members were involved in different cults or religions. How many of us have had the wrong thinking that
if we studied the other world views or beliefs, we'd be
able to either debate or dissuade our loved ones or friends
from following something other than Christianity?

Realizing the overwhelming amount of resource
materials that are in the world today, as well as the
amount of time and effort it would take to digest all this

information, we can feel ill-equipped at best due to a lack of knowledge. And a lack of knowledge of the right thing —the word of God—will directly impact our level of confidence in God, which will result in a loss of boldness and confidence in the demonstration power of the gospel.

On the surface, the desire to study other cults or religions may sound fine, even commendable. However, I think this is just another tactic of the devil to deceive believers. Why on earth would you want to spend time studying counterfeit teachings of the Bible? It won't give you a greater understanding of the truth. It doesn't fit in with Paul's instruction in Philippians 4:8-9 telling us to think on things that are true, honest, just, pure, lovely and of good report. And it diverts your own attention away from the simplicity of the gospel.

> But I fear, lest by any means, as the serpent beguiled Eve through his subtlety, so your minds should be corrupted from *the simplicity that is in Christ.* (2 Cor 11:3, emphasis added)

When I was in my early twenties, working in Illinois, I was taught how to quickly recognize a counterfeit $20 bill by studying the real thing—special markings, threads, coloring, etc. After spending so much time on the real deal, I could easily spot the phony. It works the same way with Christianity. When you learn the real thing, who Jesus is and what his word says, then you can easily spot the other counterfeit religions. The devil comes as an angel of light, and his job is to get you to take your eyes off Jesus. What better way than to get people to try to spend so much time studying the fakes, that they don't spend time in the Bible! Pretty sneaky, huh?

Christianity is the only faith where people need to place their trust in a savior, Jesus Christ, and not in themselves, in order to be restored back into a right relationship with God. Remember, no matter who is attempting to sway you or convince you that they've got the real thing, unless they believe that Jesus IS God, that he ROSE from the dead, that he IS ALIVE today, and only through HIS BLOOD (not works of the law or the flesh) can they be made the righteousness of God, then all they have is wishful thinking.

Righteous Indignation   *Mark & Denise*

Sometimes it takes a violent determination to appropriate the things of God into our lives. This is what Jesus meant in Matt 11:12 when he said that the kingdom of heaven suffers violence and the violent take it by force. You need to get to the point where you are fed up with your situation and prepared to do whatever it takes to get rid of it and keep it from coming back.

When we are sick, how comfortable are we with our sickness? Is it something we are just used to ? Is it something we are willing to put up with, or would we rather die than remain in it? The question is how intolerant of our situation are we, and how ready are we to be rid of it? Would you rather die than live another day without the answer, or are you waiting for the answer to come on you from the outside?

When we were born again, we received our healing as a spiritual reality along with everything else that is God's will for us. The next step is to promote the manifestation of that healing in our body. How do we do this? The first and foremost thing is to act on the God-given authority you have as a child of God and command your body to line up with the word of God. Command the sickness, the pain, the affliction in your body to leave. Yes, we are saying to actually speak to the affected part of your body. You have the name of Jesus, so use it! Don't take no for an answer.

A lot of times when we feel sick, our body rebels at what we say. But does our body have authority over our spirit? No, it doesn't. Our spirit has authority over our body, but only as the mind is renewed to the reality in the spirit. That means you command your body according to what you believe. The grace of God already provided for our healing, and it's our faith—our corresponding action of what we believe—that brings that manifestation into existence. Sometimes that has to be violent and aggressive. *It is not a passive thing to receive from God.* We can't just sit back and wait for it to drop onto us.

Jesus said to the paralytic man they let down through the roof, "Pick up your bed and walk." That meant the man had to do something. The man with the withered hand in the synagogue to whom Jesus said, "Stretch forth your hand", had to do something. The blind man on the side of the road as Jesus was passing by was not passive about his healing. In fact, everyone around him was telling him to shut up. But he cried the more loudly, "Jesus, son of David, have mercy on me." These people were all active in receiving their healing.

Denise spoke to a woman in her seventies who had heard Andrew Wommack teach about speaking to your mountain (infirmity); she thought he was crazy. She had been diagnosed with rheumatoid arthritis for over 15 years and had been unable to move without either someone's assistance or a walker. After hearing the truth about the power of God, this woman determined that every day she would take some time to command her knees to be pain free and her feet to take her where she wanted to go. Three days had passed and nothing *seemed* to be happening to her body. But she said, "Something on the inside of me said I was doing the right thing, and to keep speaking to my body." Around the seventh day, she was completely healed and didn't need any help or even a cane to get around! She had chosen to believe and act on her faith.

If you are in need of healing, we would ask one question: *How active are you in receiving your healing?* The healing has already been given to you. It's already yours. This is the last day you have to suffer with it, if you start acting like you believed you already received it.

Righteousness – Not By The Law   *Mark*

> *Whosoever therefore shall break one of these least
> commandments, and shall teach men so, he shall
> be called the least in the kingdom of heaven: but
> whosoever shall do and teach them, the same shall
> be called great in the kingdom of heaven. For I say
> unto you, That except your righteousness shall
> exceed the righteousness of the scribes and Phari-
> sees, ye shall in no case enter into the kingdom of
> heaven.* (Matthew 5:19-20)

*Q. Where does the above verse leave the believer who is
not trusting in his own righteousness or holiness, but in
Jesus?*

A. This passage isn't as much about keeping the commandments as it is about being righteous before God.
According to the Old Testament law, if God's people kept
the commandments, he promised to bless, multiply, sustain and protect them. However, the righteousness that
Jesus was talking about in Matthew 5:20 is a quality of
righteousness that is better than doing everything right.
And it's just plain impossible to achieve. A person cannot
ever obtain it by keeping the law because actions do not
change the nature of the spirit.

That was the problem with the scribes and Pharisees.
Because God had commanded the Law, they thought that
acting right made them right in the sight of God. But it
didn't change their inner nature. They did everything
right and still were all wrong. If you doubt that, go read
the twenty-third chapter of Matthew, where Jesus absolutely rips their charade apart. The only thing he left

them with was the choice to either repent or kill him off. We know what they chose.

But, even so, we can't just throw away Jesus' validation of the law in verse 19. What does this mean to us if we are trusting in Jesus instead of our works? Is it true that we still need to keep the law to be justified? Just a little earlier, in Matthew 5:17, Jesus said he didn't come to destroy the law, but to fulfill it. But Colossians 2:14 says that the handwriting of ordinances that was against us has been blotted out, taken out of the way, and nailed to the cross. This refers to the commandments and makes it pretty clear that the law doesn't exist anymore—it has been destroyed.

Because of this apparent contradiction, people can and did get really confused. Even the early church struggled with keeping the law after Jesus was resurrected. "Sure," they said, "we've been forgiven, but we still have to keep the commandments, don't we?" *Don't we?* Most of the writings of the apostle Paul addressed this very question.

There is a great example of this problem in the fifteenth chapter of the book of Acts. The passage is about a group of people in the Jerusalem church who were arguing that Gentile converts needed to keep the law in order to be saved. James, the head of the church, ultimately made this determination and wrote it to be delivered by the hands of Barnabas and Paul:

> For it seemed good to the Holy Ghost, and to us, to lay upon you no greater burden than these necessary things; That ye abstain from meats offered to idols, and from blood, and from things strangled, and from fornication: from which if ye

keep yourselves, ye shall do well. Fare ye well.
(Acts 15:28-29)

If you just took that one statement and compared it to
what Jesus said in Matthew 5:19, then James is going to
be called least in the kingdom of heaven. James has just
instructed the church *not* to keep the whole law! "It's
alright, folks, don't worry about it. You don't have to
show up for the feasts, you don't have to wear the psal-
teries and fringes. It's not a problem if you're not circum-
cised, you can pretty much eat what you want, you don't
have to send a tenth of your stuff to the temple. You
don't need to be Jewish. Just watch these four areas and
you'll be fine . . . " And to top it off, he said the Holy
Ghost was behind it.

So, going back to Matthew 5, what was Jesus saying?
Obviously, there's a big contradiction in scripture if there
isn't something else at stake. But there is. If you read on
down past verse 20, Jesus begins to make a series of state-
ments about the law as it related to what was in the heart.
For instance, in verses 21-24, he quotes the law that said,
"Thou shalt not kill"; and then says it's just as bad if
you're mad at somebody without a cause. In verse 28, he
says looking at a woman with lust is the same as committing adultery with her.

In the following verses, he actually starts to contradict
what the law said. "You heard it said that you need to
perform your oaths to God? I'm telling you not to make
any oaths at all. Eye for an eye, tooth for a tooth? Don't
seek revenge, let them have more than what they want.
Love your enemies instead of hating them; that's how
God is." (vvs. 33-34, 38–41, 43-45, paraphrased)

The main principle that Jesus was expressing is that righteousness—true right standing before God—is separate from the works of the law. Even though the law reflects what is right, simply keeping it doesn't separate you from the desire to break it.

I'll give a personal example of my own. The speed limit on the rural road in front of my house is 45 mph. It's usually empty, it's straight and it's at least five miles long. I've gotten more than one speeding ticket on this road. Why? Because I have a desire in me to go a lot faster than the boring old legal limit. And even when I set my car on cruise control, and technically am keeping the law, I still have to fight that desire to step on the pedal. The solution to the problem isn't through keeping the law, although it may serve as far as the police are concerned. The solution really is in changing the desire to speed. (Hey, I'm working on it!) So, keeping the law isn't the way to be right, at least not where your motives are concerned.

That's what Jesus was saying. Paul, in his letters, says the same thing. The grace of God, through faith in Jesus, has imparted to our spirits *the righteousness of God*. Our righteousness really does exceed the righteousness of the Pharisees, because it is the same righteousness Jesus has. Furthermore, this righteousness begins to produce in us the supernatural ability to act as Jesus acted, from a motivation of love for God and love for people. That is what all the commandments are founded upon.

But, anyone who teaches that this type of righteousness comes from the law has taken themselves out from under the grace of God (Gal 5:4). It is for that reason that we would never back off from the position that we are saved apart from our actions. This is not negotiable with us. We are not made righteous by what we do.

Salvation Assurance   Denise & Mark

Q. How can I really be sure that once I've accepted Jesus, I won't lose my salvation? I mean, I've prayed for other things and haven't seen them come to pass. Is salvation like that?

A. The only way to know anything for sure is to find out what God's word says about it. And then believe it. This is the extremely simple condition God puts on us: If we confess that Jesus is our Lord, and believe he rose from the dead, we will be saved (Romans 10:9). In John 6:37, Jesus said, "All that the Father giveth me shall come to me; and him that cometh to me I will in no wise cast out." If you believe that and you come to him, you can be assured that he is not going to cast you out! But you have to believe it.

Once you place your trust in Jesus, according to Romans 8:17, you immediately become an heir of God, and a joint-heir with Christ. At some point, Satan will probably attempt to convince you that nothing really happened. After all, you don't *see* the transformation that takes place in your spirit—how it goes from being separated from God to becoming one with him (1 Cor 6:17). You don't *see* your spirit becoming sealed with the Holy Ghost (Eph 1:13, 4:30); you don't *see* the change of going from having the devil as your father (John 8:44; Eph 2:3) to having God as your father; and you don't *see* your sins completely removed (Psa 103:12). You may not even *feel* a thing when you confess Jesus as the Lord of your life.

It's different when it comes to praying for miracles that you can see, like healing or finances, for instance. If we don't see immediate answers to our prayers, we can think that maybe our prayers don't work. Therefore, maybe our prayer for salvation didn't work, maybe we're not saved. That's what human logic would say. But that kind of logic is based only on physical reality, and not on God's word.

On the other hand, it may be a real blessing that we can't always see spiritual realities, particularly as unbelievers. We have no earthly idea of how bad we looked in the spirit before we got saved. If we did, it would be just as hard to receive salvation from God as any physical miracle. If our senses were filled with the picture of evil, death, depravity and corruption that was in our spirits prior to being born again, it would be difficult to believe that even God could save us. With that in mind, it just seems to make sense that the only miracle that is eternal is also the only one you can't see.

Your salvation is an invisible, supernatural thing and is not based on your five physical senses. It's based on having faith in God. All of God's promises, including receiving Jesus as your Lord, are based on faith. You may wake up one morning and not even *feel* saved, but that doesn't make God's word any less true. Scripture says that if you believe on Jesus you will have eternal life (John 3:15,16; Rom 6:23; Rom 10:9). And since faith comes by hearing the word of God (Rom 10:17), you need to read your Bible, and hear it for yourself.

In John 10:28-29, Jesus says, "And I give unto them eternal life; and they shall never perish, neither shall any man pluck them out of my hand. My Father, which gave them me, is greater than all; and no man is able to pluck them out of my Father's hand." The word *pluck* means to take by force. That should give you an idea of how good of a grip God has on the situation. Your salvation is not so fragile that you have it one minute and lose it the next.

However, Satan will attempt to plant thoughts in your mind to get you to doubt your salvation. That's why it's so important to get this issue resolved in your own mind. He doesn't want anyone to have a relationship with God, let alone a close one. And if he can't keep you from accepting Jesus, he'll try to get you so busy doubting if you're saved or not, that you'll run yourself ragged trying to please God.

So don't doubt in the dark, what God has promised you in the light. The one thing you can be confident of is this: Since no amount of good works got you saved, no amount of wrong actions or lack of good works will remove the eternal life that has been given to you. Your righteousness is a gift from God (Rom 5:18, 6:23; Eph 2:8). A gift isn't earned, it's not bought, it's just received with thanks. As our good friend Lawson Perdue says, "Either your spirit is 100% saved, or your spirit is 100% lost; either you're 100% a child of God or you're 100% a child of the devil." You need to know which side of the fence you are on!

Saul's Troubling Spirit   Mark

There is a pervasive idea in the body of Christ that God actually causes bad things to come upon people. We know from James 1:13 that God does not test or try any of us with evil, and that only good and perfect gifts come from him (Jas 1:17). Still, people have a tendency to want to put it off on God when bad things happen.

One familiar example that we've heard people give in an attempt to prove that "God's gonna getcha" is from the book of 1 Samuel chapter 16. This has to do with Saul's troubling spirit. As the account goes, Saul, the king of Israel, had disobeyed some specific directions given by God, causing God to remove the anointing of his Spirit from Saul and place it on David. 1 Samuel 16:14 reads like this: "But the Spirit of the LORD departed from Saul, and an evil spirit from the LORD troubled him." It says *distressing* spirit in the *New King James Version*, and the *Young's Literal Translation* reads this way: "and a spirit of sadness from Jehovah terrified him." What's going on here? How can we harmonize this with the God of love we see in the New Testament?

There are two possible explanations for this. The first is that it was indeed an evil, demonic spirit that was able to influence Saul's life because the protective hand of God's Spirit had been taken from him. Looking at it in this light, God can be said to have given him that spirit, but only in a passive sense. In other words, God wasn't actively sending a devil to torment him. To say otherwise is to give substance to the idea that God uses the devil as an errand boy. That's nonsense. Look at the example of Jesus. He said, "If you've seen me, you've seen the

Father." (John 14:9) We cannot conceive of Jesus using an evil spirit to terrify someone. It's simply not compatible with what we know about Jesus, who, after all, is the perfect representation of God. So if it was an evil spirit, it was "allowed" to have influence in Saul's life because the Spirit of God was no longer upon him.

The other explanation for this is that it was actually an angel that caused Saul torment. In our everyday life, we can think of examples where evil people have been distressed by the presence of godly people. So, it's conceivable that it was actually an angelic being that, because of its holy nature, caused all of this turmoil in Saul. In this context, *evil*, *distressing*, and *troubling* are words that refer to the effect this being had on Saul, and do not refer to an aspect of its nature. This explanation fits in more closely with *Young's* translation. Scripture states in 1 Samuel 16:23 that whenever David played his harp or instrument, the troubling spirit left. If it was an angelic being, it seems likely that it would have joined David in praising God, to the point that even Saul was refreshed.

Whichever explanation is correct, this passage does not prove that God causes bad things in people's lives. Taking his Spirit from Saul does not at all mean that God had stopped loving him. But, because of Saul's inconsistency and disobedience, the change of leadership had to happen. In our opinion, it is probable that the first explanation is the more likely one, given Saul's increasing tendency to evil actions.

Slain In The Spirit   Mark & Denise

Slain in the spirit. That's a strange phrase, and it's
not even found in the Bible. Some people call it "falling
under the power". That term is more accurate, but the
question is whether or not this is a genuine physical manifestation of the power of God, or something we work up
ourselves. It could be either, depending on the person!

Actually, we can find several scriptural references for
being "slain" in the spirit or people falling to the ground
from being in the presence of God (2 Chron 5:14; Ezek
1:28; 3:23; Dan 8:17; 10:8; Acts 9:4; 26:14; Rev 1:17).
When Jesus was arrested in the garden of Gethsemane,
the soldiers who came to take him all fell backward when
Jesus declared, "I AM". If there was any doubt about it,
this should be a powerful indication that no flesh can
withstand the power of God!

We've experienced this ourselves in the past, and also
have seen people go down under the power when we pray
for them. However, in charismatic circles this seems to
have become almost a religious practice, or as a friend of
ours, Clifton Coulter, calls it—a "courtesy drop". Some
ministers even push!

When we were in Dublin on a ministry trip with
Andrew Wommack, Dave Duell, and Wendell Parr, after
Wendell finished his message, people came forward for
prayer. Mark and I went to pray for a certain man who,
compared to my 5'4" frame seemed like a hulk—taller and
bigger. He apparently had constant severe pain in his
body that he said was a result of a genetic condition. It
was something that he had suffered with for a very long

time. I didn't know this at the time, but while I was binding the spirit that was afflicting him, at that same exact moment, Mark was commanding it to leave. The result was that this fellow shot back against some folding chairs and hit the concrete floor on his backside. I was thinking, *God, please don't let this guy be hurt or mad at us for landing on the floor.* Instead, he shook his head, looked amazed, and the first words out of his mouth were, "The pain is completely gone!"

This guy did not turn around before we prayed for him to see if there were ushers (which there weren't), and he didn't stop to see if he'd hit anything if he fell (which he did). He simply received the transference of the power of God with immediate results.

So, the bottom line is that if you want to find out for sure whether this is a genuine manifestation of the Holy Ghost or not, you may want to consider having an altar call without ushers to catch! If someone looks around before they are prayed for to see if there are ushers there, they might be expecting to fall down simply out of courtesy to tradition.

Sowing And Reaping   Denise & Mark

But this I say, He which soweth sparingly shall reap also sparingly; and he which soweth bountifully shall reap also bountifully. (2 Corinthians 9:6)

For as the rain cometh down, and the snow from heaven, and returneth not thither, but watereth the earth, and maketh it bring forth and bud, that it may give seed to the sower, and bread to the eater: (Isaiah 55:10)

Now he that ministereth seed to the sower both minister bread for your food, and multiply your seed sown, and increase the fruits of your righteousness; (2 Corinthians 9:10)

Be not deceived; God is not mocked: for whatsoever a man soweth, that shall he also reap. For he that soweth to his flesh shall of the flesh reap corruption; but he that soweth to the Spirit shall of the Spirit reap life everlasting. And let us not be weary in well doing: for in due season we shall reap, if we faint not. (Galatians 6:7-9)

Have you ever noticed that God is a God of multiplication? Throughout the word we see God has spoken things to be multiplied, such as his word, his people, the disciples, fruit of the trees, grace, peace, love and even our finances. When God created the world and man, he set up seed systems that would propagate themselves. He doesn't have to keep making mankind because it's based on the man's seed. He doesn't have to keep making trees, because they produce their own seeds which in turn bring forth more of their own kind.

In the parable of the sower (Matt 13:18; Mark 4:3; Luke 8:5), Jesus says the seed being sown is the word of God (Luke 8:11). The different types of ground are the different conditions of how sensitive our heart is to God. We need to sow what his word says into our hearts and stay sensitive.

Prosperity is also based on sowing and reaping. If you sow seed into a field, you'll reap a harvest from that field. If you don't sow any seed in that field, you won't produce a crop. It's not the seed's fault or the ground's fault. The person who sows the seed needs to be responsible to sow into good ground, be consistent, and know that the harvest comes in due season. As long as you sow, you will reap.

Another aspect to the financial area is that prosperity has some time factors involved in it. Much like any agricultural system, there is time between the sowing and the reaping. Farmers understand this as a matter of course, but when it comes to money we forget it's the same principle involved. We put a financial seed into something, and we expect the harvest by tomorrow. It would be there tomorrow if we had sown that seed months ago. We look at the physical field of dirt and we understand about the time factor, but we are curiously blind about money. It's the same system. You can't cheat the system of agriculture and make the seeds into a harvest overnight.

God can and will do miracles for us where money is concerned, but the principle of sowing and reaping, of like producing like, has been around since the third day of creation. That is how the whole kingdom works. It's ". . . as if a man should cast seed into the ground, and should sleep, and rise night and day, and the seed should spring and grow up, he knoweth not how." (Mark 4:26-27) The earth brings forth the fruit; our job is to keep planting the seed. If we will stay consistent with our planting, over and over, time after time, then our harvest will keep coming, over and over, time after time. We're not planting into a physical field that is subject to a cold barren winter; the growing season for this isn't affected by the natural realm.

So if you don't see prosperity in your daily life, it's not because of God. His word will always accomplish its purpose, but it is up to us to keep the soil of our hearts sensitive to God.

Tribulations   *Mark*

*Wherefore I desire that ye faint not at my
tribulations for you, which is your glory.*
(Ephesians 3:13)

*Confirming the souls of the disciples, and
exhorting them to continue in the faith, and
that we must through much tribulation enter
into the kingdom of God.* (Acts 14:22)

I read something by an author on the internet (I
know, I know, I should know better) who wrote that if
you didn't embrace tribulation, you were embracing a
"false doctrine"—namely, that Jesus came to redeem us
from suffering. The two verses above were part of his
scriptural evidence. We heard Mother Theresa say pretty
much the same thing. It sounded as if people want to
believe that there is a redeeming quality to trials and
temptations, even an exultation in undergoing the worst
that life or God or the devil can throw at us—although
there seems to be very little discernment about the source
of the trials. We even heard a guy say that his friend was
rejoicing because God had accounted him "worthy"
enough to give him cancer. We wouldn't be surprised to
find out that God has a little flat spot on his forehead
from hitting himself in disbelief over some of the stupid
things we say!

Concerning Ephesians 3:13 and Acts 14:22, Amer-
icans have very little conception of what Paul meant by
"suffering". From our experience in ministering to
thousands of people in the United States, most prayer

requests fall into three main categories: healing, finances, and relationships. Don't misunderstand me—those are serious issues, but it's not the suffering that Paul was talking about. What he was referring to was the persecution he suffered because of the gospel he preached. This is from *Adam Clarke's Commentary* on Ephesians 3:13:

> Verse 13. [I desire that ye faint not...] In those primitive times, when there was much persecution, people were in continual danger of falling away from the faith who were not well grounded in it. This the apostle deprecates, and advances a strong reason why they should be firm: "I suffer my present imprisonment on account of demonstrating your privileges, of which the Jews are envious: I bear my afflictions patiently, knowing that what I have advanced is of God, and thus I give ample proof of the sincerity of my own conviction. The sufferings, therefore, of your apostles are honourable to you and to your cause; and far from being any cause why you should faint, or draw back like cowards, in the day of distress, they should be an additional argument to induce you to persevere." (emphasis added)

I heard awhile back, before the overthrow of communism in Russia, that it was a common practice to have a prospective disciple memorize five or six scriptures about persecution before they ever prayed to receive Jesus as Lord. The rationale was this: you should know these verses before you become a Christian, because it truly could cost you your life. Yet, by all accounts, those believers put us to shame in terms of their steadfastness, their level of joy and their intimacy of relationship with God and each other.

Andrew Wommack gave a testimony about a couple he met in Czechoslovakia whose walls inside their house were covered with ice because the government shut their heat off. Their diet consisted of lard on bread, and they were incredulous at Andrew's suggestion that they might leave and move to the States. "Why would we leave what God is doing here?" They were full of joy and happy to be suffering on account of the gospel. That's what Paul was talking about—suffering abuse at the hands of people actively rejecting God—suffering because he was a Christian.

To equate this type of suffering with a "spiritual test" is missing the point, particularly if one means to say that God gives us these so-called tests to prove our character. It is hardly a fair comparison to say that poverty or a terminal illness is the same as being thrown to the lions or being burned alive because of what we believe. Indeed, we should lay down our lives and pick up our cross daily, but that does not mean that we should embrace those things that are categorized in terms of "the curse of the law". God forbid that I should ever accuse him of testing me with something from which he has already redeemed me with his own blood. "Carrying the cross" means that I should be crucifying my own self-centeredness, not paying my way into heaven as a victim of Satan.

Is it a "false doctrine" to say that Jesus redeemed us from suffering? No, it's not. It's not false to say Jesus suffered rejection from God so we don't have to; he suffered the penalty of our sin so that we don't have to; he suffered the curse of the law so that we don't have to. But I will admit that he did not save us from persecution, because that concerns the free will of our fellow man.

God doesn't override anybody's will so that we can have a free ride.*

Psalm 34:19 says, "Many are the afflictions of the righteous: but the LORD delivereth him out of them all." So if the Lord does the delivering and is the source of our relief, then he is not the one causing the afflictions.

All that being said, there are tribulations associated with the life we live on this earth. And yes, there are tests and trials. And in those times we have opportunity to show God's faithfulness. Paul said we should rejoice in tribulation and he's right; but he also said we should rejoice always. That is the main thing, I think; not going forth welcoming the bad; but knowing at all times the love of the Father will bring us through because he is faithful.

*Denise has written more about this topic.
(See *Persecution—A Sound Word, Volume 1*)

Types Of Baptisms   *Mark & Denise*

In asking people if they have ever received the baptism of the Holy Ghost, we receive a lot of replies of "Yes, I've been water baptized." But that's not we were asking. We see three main types of baptisms in the Bible: baptism into the body of Christ, water baptism and the baptism of the Holy Ghost. We also see three parts to any baptism: the thing that gets baptized, the element that the thing is baptized into, and the one who puts the thing into the element.

First, there is the new birth, where the person is baptized into the body of Christ (Gal 3:27; Eph 4:5; 1 Cor 12:13). This is the baptism that saves you. The only person capable of performing that baptism is God. The apostle Paul wrote in 2 Corinthians 5:17: "Therefore if any man be in Christ, he is a new creature: old things are passed away; behold, all things are become new." The *new creature* is the real you that is identical to the Spirit of Christ (Rom 8:9).

Second, there is a water baptism, where the person gets immersed into the water. The word *baptize* is from the Greek word *baptizo* which means to immerse or make fully wet. Water baptism can be performed by a minister, pastor, or any believer, like Philip in Acts 8:38. Unlike what some denominations believe, this baptism does not have a recreative or saving function, but is useful as a point of reference for identifying with the death, burial, and resurrection of Jesus with our immersion into water and rising up in the newness of the life of Christ. Since Jesus is our example and he was water baptized (Matt 3:15; Mark 1:9; Luke 3:21), we are also commanded to be water baptized (Matt 28:19). Like receiving salvation, the decision to be water baptized must be made by the individual. So this would not apply to a newborn baby or child who is too young to understand the significance.

Third, there is the baptism of the Holy Ghost where the baptizer is Jesus and the element is the Holy Ghost (John 1:33; Matt 3:11; Acts 1:5). Jesus had commanded the disciples to wait in Jerusalem until they were endued with power from on high (Luke 24:49). This is that which was spoken by the prophet Joel. The baptism of the Holy Spirit is available to *every* believer so that they can demonstrate God's love with signs and wonders for his glory. (See *Baptism Of The Holy Ghost—A Sound Word, Volume 1*).

> And it shall come to pass in the last days, saith God, I will pour out of my Spirit upon all flesh: and your sons and your daughters shall prophesy, and your young men shall see visions, and your old men shall dream dreams: And on my servants and on my handmaidens I will pour out in those days of my Spirit; and they shall prophesy. (Acts 2:17-18; Joel 2:28-29)

War And God's Will   *Mark*

Q. The Bible tells us that there will be wars and rumors of wars. As believers, should we pray for the war (in Iraq) *to stop? How do we pray? Does God approve of wars?*

A. Wars are destructive; therefore, they are not God's best for mankind. Every effort should be made to live in peace with all men. However, evil men do exist and, to the extent that they refuse to restrain themselves, God is for the destruction of that evil. If it takes a war to accomplish that task, it is a just war in God's eyes. In the Old Testament, God commanded the destruction of individuals and nations at the hand of Israel because of their stand against God's covenant people. He hasn't changed in this respect. He is patient and does not destroy things out of hand. He was even willing to spare the cities of Sodom and Gomorrah had there been any righteous people in them. That's why this country isn't destroyed, because of us, his children. But, ultimately, if his mercy and grace are not received, destruction is inevitable.

We should pray for this war to stop. But not for anything short of its desired end—the destruction of an evil murderous regime. Pray for all men everywhere that light overcomes the darkness (it always does—John 1:5), that evil men are cut off and destroyed (Psa 10:15; 34:16), that the righteous are delivered from evil (Psa 140:1; Matt 6:13), and that the light of the gospel will be preached and have entrance into the minds of those who have not believed (2 Cor 4:4). In particular, keep praying for the peace of Jerusalem. That peace ultimately will not be achieved until Jesus sits on his throne in that city.

Why Do Bad Things Happen? Mark & Denise

The things that happen in the earth are a result of the fall of man—that is the event that produced sickness, disease, murder, war, accidents, etc. If you don't know God's true character of love, you may even want to lump the reason for these "bad things" into a category called "the sovereignty of God". He's often given credit for the bad stuff, along with the good stuff, because he's often thought of as always directly intervening in every one of man's affairs.

You cannot assume that every sickness man gets is because he is sinful or separated from God (especially in the case of believers). Sickness exists in our fallen world, and it is likely that each of us can or may become susceptible to some type of sickness or disease at some time or another in our lives. When sickness comes to attack us, God's word says we *were* healed. But if we don't equip ourselves with the knowledge of our authority or our ability to act in the name of Jesus, it's not God's fault. The word says in Hosea 4:6 that God's people perish for lack of knowledge. Another way you could say it is, God's children are destroyed because they reject his word.

For example, when diseases are spread by homosexual contact, that's not the result of God's judgment against homosexuality or else every single homosexual would have the same diseases. Rather, when homosexuals (or even heterosexuals) continue to sin, they take a risk every time they have sex. It is a risk associated with the choice of lifestyle.

Diseases exist in the world as tangible effects of biological organisms. The living things in this world are affected as a result of the fall of man. Throughout the history of the earth, there have been plagues (bubonic plague, AIDS in Africa, etc.) that are *not* the result of God's judgment, but are the result of unsanitary living, wrong lifestyle practices, etc.

The biblical point of view is that we are living in an age where God's grace toward mankind is shown through the atoning death of Jesus, though the earth is still suffering from the fall of man. Mankind either accepts or rejects this sacrifice for sin; but that doesn't take everything bad out of the world. God does intervene in human affairs, but primarily for the purpose of blessing people rather than dispensing judgment for their sins. Their actions have already been dealt with on the cross.

Accidents? They can happen from carelessness or ignorance, from making wrong choices, from being in the wrong place at the wrong time, or they can occur unexpectedly without any intent. For example, if a person speeds, loses control of the car and drives off a cliff, that is not God's fault, nor is it God's judgment on that person. That is simply the bad judgment of the driver. If someone is about to get in a car accident, God won't stop the law of gravity to save that person, only to allow the rest of the population to fall off the face of the earth. If someone chooses unwisely to be a drunk driver, God cannot override their free will and stop them, regardless of the possible disastrous consequences.

We can see God's true character, goodness and mercy revealed through his word. We see God as our heavenly Father. James 1:13-17 tells us that God cannot be tempted, nor does he tempt man with evil; and only that which is good and perfect comes from him. Psalm 145 is just one example of God's goodness and mercy expressed in the word. Jesus is an example of God's goodness and mercy expressed in the flesh; and Jesus didn't go around causing bad things to happen.

Why Was I Created? *Denise*

Thou art worthy, O Lord, to receive glory and honour and power: for thou hast created all things, and for thy pleasure they are and were created. (Revelation 4:11)

When I was young I remember asking my mom why was I born. It seems I couldn't have been more than eight or nine years old, but at that age you have a lot of time on your hands to think about things. Mom looked at me, sort of laughed and said something like, "There's no reason. You live, you die and that's about it." I went up to my room feeling pretty bummed out from that answer. I mean, if I was only around eight, I still had a lot of years ahead of me. There had to be something bigger for my life than my own house, which was a bit chaotic.

God seemed so far away up there in the sky, and I had never even heard of a personal relationship with Jesus. I had religion books in school, went to church every Sunday, went to confession, but knew there had to be more. There always seemed to be an empty place in me that over the years I had unsuccessfully tried to fill with everything but Jesus. I wish I knew then what I began to learn when I was about to turn 30—that I could put my complete trust and hope in Jesus, and he would never leave me or disappoint me.

Priorities shift after you get saved, and mine took a 180 degree turn. In fact, there was so much initial change in me that my family and friends thought I had joined a cult. Like the song by Carmen, you could say I got "radically saved". They liked the "old Denise" better. But I didn't and figured God didn't either. For me to make decisions based on what God thought was a tough pill for them to swallow. Where was the Denise they grew up with? It was strange that finally after 30 years I had begun to live my life with Jesus as my first priority, and they didn't like it one bit. But it didn't matter to me really. I've discovered that God is more than enough, and I was created to glorify him, to honor him, and to know that no matter what happens in my life, forever I'll still be praising him! I have all of God's love, power, joy, peace, and faith on the inside of me—priceless.

Wouldn't it be a thrill for a parent to hear their child, instead of constantly asking for things, come into the kitchen one day and say, "Mom, will you sit at the table with me? I just want to tell you what a good mom you are. I just want to spend some time here with you." That's all God is wanting from us—to come to his table of fellowship and spend some time thanking him and letting him know what a good God he is. God knows you perfectly and loves you perfectly. He loves you no less than he loves Jesus. We were created to have that personal relationship with him because it pleased him to make us.

Women In Ministry *Denise*

The first time I was asked what I thought about women in ministry, it sort of aggravated me, and seemed like a rather biased question. Until I realized that the people who were doing the asking were all women! I was raised in a family of four sisters, who were all quite smart and capable. Growing up in the northwest suburbs of Chicago, I liked sports including football, basketball, volleyball and street hockey. Our cousins who lived down the street were mostly boys, and the teams were mainly comprised of the guys around the neighborhood.

My sisters and I all went to work at an early age, were taught how to save as well as handle our finances. My sister, Darlene, and I had jobs at AT&T for over a decade, while my oldest sister Sharon was a CPA and the comptroller of a company. Renee, who was six years older than I, could run payroll and accounting numbers backwards and forwards and also tutored me in math. I knew from working at AT&T in the 1970's and 1980's, that at that time it was pretty much a man's world in the business arena. There was rarely a woman boss, and I hated being told I couldn't get a certain promotion because I was a female. Enough said.

As I thought about the question whether women should be in ministry, it seemed as though they were only asking about the fivefold ministry i.e., apostle, prophet, evangelist, pastor and teacher. But those aren't the only valid ministries. There are women who minister in teaching, music, training, and women who minister to their families and in other ways.

So what about a woman being a pastor? First Timothy 3:2 tells us, "A bishop then must be blameless, the husband of one wife, vigilant, sober, of good behaviour, given to hospitality, apt to teach." Though it doesn't say a *pastor*, the term *bishop* is equivalent. Hey, I'm all for women having equal rights, but I also know a woman can't be the husband of one wife! On the other hand, is it better to have a woman in a pastoral position than to have a flock with no shepherd? If there isn't a man who is willing or able to do the job, then certainly a woman who is capable of filling that position should do so.

Andrew Wommack told us that he used to usher at Katherine Kuhlman meetings and she used to say that God had asked four other men to minister before he asked her. They all said no. She said she was God's fifth pick.

Am I saying women are not important? Absolutely not. Who was the first to see Jesus raised from the dead? A woman. Who told the disciples about the resurrection?

The same woman. There were many effective women in the New Testament including Anna, Aquila and Priscilla, the women who ministered to Jesus, the widow woman, Jesus' mother, Phillip's daughters, etc. Even in the Old Testament we see women who played important roles including Miriam, Rahab, Deborah and Anna. Today, we see any number of effective women ministers including Joyce Meyers, Gloria Copeland, Paula White, Marilyn Hickey, and Denise Renner to name a few.

However, just looking at the way things are, on the whole, men usually don't prefer a woman ministering to them. I'm not talking about husband and wife *teams*, such as the Copelands, who have both men and women in attendance. But, if we look at a Joyce Meyers or Paula White conference, for example, the attendees are predominantly women. You probably won't see a woman holding a men's meeting. It seems that, all things being equal, women will respond to a minister of either sex better than a man will.

Paul began his salutations in the book of Galatians with, "Paul, an apostle (not of men, neither by man, but by Jesus Christ)". Paul didn't have an official degree, wasn't a licensed minister, and didn't have an ordination ceremony in a Bible college. But he knew he was called and sent by God. There is no doubt that *both* men and women are called into ministry. God is the one who gives you this desire, and should be the one who opens this door.

But, there is also no doubt that both men and women kick their own doors open to get into ministry where they are *not* called. What should we do in that kind of a situation? As Gamaliel the Pharisee said in Acts 5:38-39:

And now I say unto you, Refrain from these men, and let them alone: for if this counsel or this work be of men, it will come to nought: But if it be of God, ye cannot overthrow it; lest haply ye be found even to fight against God.

THE STORY
BEHIND THE SONG

Already Got It

© 2002 Mark & Denise Abernethy
From *Jumping Off The Cliff*

I've already got it, not trying to
 get it
I've already got it
Jesus is come, He's in me to stay

You made me righteous
 by the blood of Your son
It's not by my works
 or what I've done
When You see me
 Your eyes see You

Eternally Yours
 too good to be true

I've already got it,
 the joy of the Lord
Not trying to get it,
 the peace of the Lord
I've already got it,
 the love the Lord
Jesus is come
 He's in me to stay

We wrote this song during Andrew Wommack's first Summer Bible Conference in Colorado Springs. He taught a series called, *You've Already Got It, Quit Trying To Get It.* I had been humming the chorus lyrics during the week and shared it with Mark who said he had been working on a chord progression with a really great groove. He said I could have it to use with my lyrics and we finished it together. He threw in a couple of good lines as well, and there you had it.

So many people are trying to get stuff from God, like his power, glory, love, joy, peace, and freedom, when all of the time, it's right there on the inside of your born-again spirit according to Galatians 5:25. Instead of trying to get more of anything, we need to focus on learning what's been placed on the inside of us. When God looks at you, he sees himself—*the* Spirit of Christ in us!

We're justified by Jesus dying in our place. That means we've been made completely holy and righteous in God's eyes. How amazing is that? We've been redeemed

(Gal 3:13; 4:5; Tit 2:14; 1 Pet 1:18; Rev 5:9), meaning Jesus paid a debt that he didn't owe by shedding his blood on our account. And if that wasn't enough, we were given his delegated authority with the name of Jesus (Matt 10:1; 28:18; Luke 9:1; 10:19; John 1:12) to have power over the enemy, over sickness, and even over death. Wherever we go, we're supposed to look and act like Jesus, and operate in the same miracle-working power that he did.

Denise

TAKE A NOTE: We deliberately left out the words to the rap section of this song, because you have to hear us singing it (especially Mark) to really appreciate it! This song is on our *Jumping Off The Cliff* CD.

In A Tent

Living in a tent
but I'm longing for my home
Living in a tent
but I'm longing for my home
It's a temporary dwelling
but I'm not living here all alone

I've got me some help in here
the Father, Son & Holy Ghost,
I've got me some help in here
the Father, Son & Holy Ghost,
Sometimes I get so excited
'cause I can't tell which one
I love the most

Well it's showin' a little weather
from rain that comes
a pourin' down
But I am assured,
my stakes are secure
I pitch my tent on higher ground

Living in a tent
and I know who I'm living for
Living in a tent
and I know who I'm living for

I'll receive a home in glory
and live there with my Lord

I may be stuck in here
but my spirit man is free
I may be stuck in here
but my spirit man is free
I've got this treasure in an earthly
vessel
The life the Lord has given to me

I've got the guarantee
of your spirit
That things won't always
be this way
And I'm looking forward
with gratitude
To my own resurrection day

Living in a tent
but I'm designed for eternity
Living in a tent
but I'm designed for eternity
One day I'll fold this thing up
and you can say goodbye to me

The apostle Paul said it was better to be with the Lord, than to be here. My spirit bears witness with that, and my body is starting to come into agreement. As much as I'd like to deny the fact that this body is going to pack it in (barring the Lord's return, that is), I just can't get away from the reality that this flesh is not going to last. Probably a good thing, since it would be nasty to live in a body that keeps on getting older but never dies.

Denise provided the initial inspiration for this song with the below lyrics, and said I needed to come up with the music. Of course, that's when it became a blues tune.

> *I'm in a tent, it's a temporary dwelling*
> *My spirit man inside longing for home*
> *I'm in a tent, it's my temporary dwelling*
> *And for the things of heaven I do long*

I had the first couple stanzas and the chords for the bridge, and let the song sit for awhile. When we started in earnest to produce our *Jumping Off The Cliff* project, something real scary happened to my hearing. I lost the ability to hear the lower frequencies with my left ear; consequently everything I heard was out of balance. At times my physical balance was off, as well. It was not at all a happy experience. Especially not for a musician.

I am now healed, praise God, and the experience taught me some things about healing, faith, etc., but that's another subject for another time. However, Denise and I sat in our studio and wrote the rest of the lyrics at a time when my body was not working right. It became part of my stand of faith, actually, in that this body is temporary and therefore subject to change. For my part, I wouldn't have minded putting this body off at all. As I wrote in the song, "One day I'm gonna fold this thing up, and you can say goodbye to me." After I leave this earth, the only way you'll see me again is if you go to heaven.

Mark

TAKE A NOTE: Sure we write folk music—Chicago folk music. Mark was proud to include his son, Eric, on keyboards in the session. This song is on our *Jumping Off The Cliff* CD.

Millennial Rain

©1999 Denise & Mark Abernethy
From *Open Up The Gates!*

Walking in the millennial rain,
Walking in the millennial rain
We're drenched in God's shower
 Of demonstration power
Nothing to lose, all to gain

I'm righteous by faith in his blood
That he shed on the cross for me

Paid for our sins
Past, present, future
So we can walk in liberty

We are the children of God
Ruling and reigning with him
We are his workmanship
Servants of righteousness
Declaring the victory from sin

Regardless what millennium we're in, we know one thing: that for those of us who have taken the step of simply believing what God has said, he is ready and willing to show himself strong on our behalf. Does this song have a "hidden meaning" behind the title? Nope. We just happened to write it in 1999 during a conference with the same name. That's all. But what we do believe about the millennial rain is this: When we saturate ourselves in the knowledge of his love toward us, we become like conduits, able to release that love through us towards others which results in signs and wonders following.

We really are drenched in God's demonstration power. As a result, more miracles will be seen; more people will live in his blessings; more will be delivered from the notion that God is angry with us. More and more people will find out God is after our hearts because he truly does love us; therefore, more people will be brought into his family and kingdom. God loves us because of who HE is and what Jesus has done, not because of who we are and what WE have tried to do. This grace will offend some who believe that it's up to us to please God, but it will also draw others who learn that God is pleased with them regardless of what they've done. "For thou hast created all things, and for thy pleasure they are and were created." (Revelation 4:11) And for these things we praise our God who through his grace has extended his salvation to the whole earth.

Mark & Denise

TAKE A NOTE: A pop tune with rain, thunder and a neat horn section written during a ministry conference in 1999. Learn about walking in the authority and power that God has given us. This song is on our *Open Up The Gates!* CD.

Praise Looks Good

From *Open Up The Gates!*

Praise looks good on you
  even long into the night
Praise looks good on you
  even after a fight
It doesn't leave circles
  under your eyes
It doesn't make you want
  to tell lies
Praise looks good on you
  even after you die

Praise looks good on you,
  even long into the night
Praise looks good on you,
  even after a fight
It doesn't matter
  the color your skin
It doesn't matter
  the nation you're in
Praise looks good on you
  even after you die

Have you ever watched someone who was truly praising the Lord? Not watching someone just going through motions or getting a Holy Ghost goose bump, but watching someone who is really caught up in ministering to and rejoicing with the Lord—their facial expression, their body movement? It's like watching someone who has just received some really good news.

Years ago before I was saved, I remember the first time I walked into the local movie theater in Park Ridge, Illinois that was rented out by a church on Sundays. It was so weird because I had been brought up in a "religious" church—you know, doing all the right things for all the wrong reasons—and the thought of actually going into the movie theater with seats that rocked back and forth, seemed almost sacrilegious. It took me quite some time to get up enough nerve to venture into a place like that. I even remember talking to my sister, Darlene, who had gone a couple of times and said the people there even looked like they were having a good time singing to the music and that some of them even raised their hands during the music. She told me her in-laws attended that church, and I figured since they weren't lunatics and seemed normal to me, it couldn't be all bad.

I'd think back to the denominational church I used to attend while growing up and they had the "organ lady" who did the music at most of the services. She sang in such a high key that not only couldn't most people hit her range, but it just seemed either too creepy or too holy. I couldn't tell which. No one in the church seemed to have any kind of real joy, and I couldn't imagine God even liking that kind of music—I sure didn't. In the 70's, however, that same church progressed to having a morning guitar mass. Now, how cool was that to bring in a stringed instrument and step up the tempo with songs like, *They'll Know We Are Christians, I'll Fly Away*, and other rocking numbers (smile). On occasion I even got to sing with that group.

Which leads me back to that converted theater in 1990. One of the first things that struck me as being really different when I walked in was a guy singing a Carmen song, *Radically Saved*. I had never heard any Christian songs on the radio or on tape, and that song seemed pretty radical. It even had a good beat to it. So here was this guy singing and smiling and having a good time and getting into the song like no one I'd ever seen in a church do. It really amazed me that this person was so on fire for God, that he could be having what looked like the best time of his life singing a song that wasn't "churchy". Praise was looking good on him.

So when I wrote this song some years later, I may have been thinking about the past, or maybe about the future. Praise is timeless. Mark and I have joked around thinking about what people will do in heaven. After all,

the evangelists will be out of a job. No one will need
healing. Will pastors be needed for different denominations? Don't think so. Prophets? Could need another
profession. But just think, musicians will never be out of
a job; they'll still be doing there what they enjoy doing
here. Only better. And maybe with more time to practice. Imagine you're in heaven. Getting tired of the
choir? Go down the street for some jazz. Or how about
some symphonies? A little Bach or Beethoven perhaps?
Just visit them while you're there. Yes, praise will look
good on you, even after you die.

Denise

TAKE A NOTE: By the way, the guy singing in that theater was
Mark. Little did I know I'd not only marry him, but be teaching,
writing and singing songs with him later on in life! This song is
on our *Open Up The Gates!* CD.

Run With The Vision ©2000 Mark & Denise Abernethy

From *Open Up The Gates!*

Run with the vision
 we're running the race
Run with the vision
 Jesus setting the pace
Run with the vision
 we're running by faith
Run with the vision
 abounding in grace

I see my Father
 standing at the finish line
His face is beginning to shine
 I can hear him say, "Well done"

Run with the vision
 we're running in light
Run with the vision
 the end is in sight

We are expanding the Kingdom
 the will of the Father
 the will of the Son
Setting our eyes on the prize
 as we grab the baton

Run with the vision
 we're running the race
Run with the vision
 Jesus setting the pace

We want to encourage all of you to not grow weary in your well doing, but to keep your focus on the course set before you. As the apostle Paul said, ". . . but this one thing I do, forgetting those things which are behind, and reaching forth unto those things which are before, I press toward the mark for the prize of the high calling of God in Christ Jesus." (Phil 3:13-14) It's not how fast you run the race, but that you complete the race set before you.

While Mark was ministering in music during a church service with Dave Duell, God gave him the beginnings of this song, *Run With The Vision*. Dave and his wife, Bonnie, taught us if you don't pursue the vision, *the people* won't get it. You may have to hold onto God's vision for a long time before you see it come to pass, regardless of what others say about your vision or about you.

Let's look at what the Bible says about vision:

> And the LORD answered me, and said, Write the
> vision, and make it plain upon tables, that he may
> run that readeth it. For the vision is yet for an
> appointed time, but at the end it shall speak, and
> not lie: though it tarry, wait for it; because it will
> surely come, it will not tarry. (Habakkuk 2:2-3)

In looking at the Greek wording, I've paraphrased it to
say, "Engrave the revelation or dream that I have given to
you, plainly declare it upon tablets that he may rush and
bring speedily who calls it forth, cries it out, or proclaims
it. For the revelation or dream is for a fixed time or season, but in the end it shall blow with breath (as to fan),
and not be in vain: though it may linger, await; but most
certainly it will come and not be late."

In track and field, once the runner finishes his leg in
the race, he passes the baton to the next runner who is
already on the move as the baton is passed into his hand.
We were told that when people in track and field are in
training, some carry the baton around all day to be able to
get a good feel or grip on it, so they won't drop it in the
race. And you're trained to not look back when the baton
is passed to you because it'll cost you time. Jesus passed
the baton on to the disciples and that baton has been
passed through the centuries to this present day. It's now
our leg of the race. Make sure that you're already moving
when the baton gets into your hand.

Denise

TAKE A NOTE: Grab a baton and run the race. Our Father is
waiting at the finish line! This song is on our *Open Up The
Gates!* CD.